"*The Lost Virtue of Happiness* is ri̇c̱   s us to embrace the way of other-centered self-denial springing from the practice of God's presence and vital trust in Him."

—KENNETH BOA, PhD, DPhil;
president, Reflections Ministries;
president, Trinity House Publishers

"Myriad empirical studies underscore the fact that happiness is a highly valued virtue in our world today. This handbook to happiness begins with the ultimate biblical truth: to gain your life you need to lose it."

—LUIS BUSH, international facilitator,
Transform World Connections

The LOST VIRTUE of HAPPINESS

DISCOVERING the DISCIPLINES of the GOOD LIFE

J. P. MORELAND, PhD
KLAUS ISSLER, PhD

NAVPRESS®

BRINGING TRUTH TO LIFE

OUR GUARANTEE TO YOU

We believe so strongly in the message of our books that we are making this quality guarantee to you. If for any reason you are disappointed with the content of this book, return the title page to us with your name and address and we will refund to you the list price of the book. To help us serve you better, please briefly describe why you were disappointed. Mail your refund request to: NavPress, P.O. Box 35002, Colorado Springs, CO 80935.

The Navigators is an international Christian organization. Our mission is to reach, disciple, and equip people to know Christ and to make Him known through successive generations. We envision multitudes of diverse people in the United States and every other nation who have a passionate love for Christ, live a lifestyle of sharing Christ's love, and multiply spiritual laborers among those without Christ.

NavPress is the publishing ministry of The Navigators. NavPress publications help believers learn biblical truth and apply what they learn to their lives and ministries. Our mission is to stimulate spiritual formation among our readers.

ISBN 1-57683-648-7

Cover design by Wes Youssi, The DesignWorks Group, Inc., www.thedesignworksgroup.com
Cover photo by Istock
Creative Team: Don Simpson, Arvid Wallen, Amy Spencer, Cara Iverson, Glynese Northam,
    Pat Reinheimer

Some of the anecdotal illustrations in this book are true to life and are included with the permission of the persons involved. All other illustrations are composites of real situations, and any resemblance to people living or dead is coincidental.

Unless otherwise identified, all Scripture quotations in this publication are taken from the HOLY BIBLE: NEW INTERNATIONAL VERSION® (NIV®). Copyright © 1973, 1978, 1984 by International Bible Society. Used by permission of Zondervan Publishing House. All rights reserved. Other versions used include: the *New American Standard Bible* (NASB), © The Lockman Foundation 1960, 1962, 1963, 1968, 1971, 1972, 1973, 1975, 1977, 1995; the *King James Version* (KJV); and *Today's New International® Version* (TNIV)®. Copyright 2001, 2005 by International Bible Society®. All rights reserved worldwide.

Moreland, James Porter, 1948-
  The lost virtue of happiness : discovering the disciplines of the good
life / J.P. Moreland and Klaus Issler.
    p. cm.
  Includes bibliographical references.
  ISBN 1-57683-648-7
  1. Christian life. 2. Happiness–Religious aspects–Christianity. I.
Issler, Klaus Dieter. II. Title.
  BV4501.3.M6675 2005
  248.4–dc22
                              2005015996

Printed in the United States of America

1 2 3 4 5 6 / 10 09 08 07 06

To Bill Roth
Wise counselor, solid friend

The meaning of earthly existence lies not,
as we have grown used to thinking, in prospering . . .
but in the development of the soul.

ALEKSANDR I. SOLZHENITSYN

CONTENTS

ACKNOWLEDGMENTS

WE'RE GRATEFUL FOR THE WONDERFUL EDITING DON SIMPSON did to help our ideas shine through more clearly. We would also like to thank our wives, Hope Moreland and Beth Issler, for their helpful feedback and support for this project. I (J. P.) want to thank my therapist, Dr. Christopher Linamen, for seeking the kingdom, loving me, and being excellent at what he does. Further, each of us received funds for writing from EIDOS Christian Center, and we are most grateful for this aid. Finally, we are thankful to God for each other. We have been friends and fellow soldiers for twenty-five years, and it was great joy to write this book together.

CHAPTER ONE

TODAY'S CONFUSION
ABOUT HAPPINESS

WE HAVE FORGOTTEN HOW TO LIVE LIFE.

I (J. P.) don't mean that we're not active, involved with friends, busy at work. I don't mean that we're not spending time with family, meeting with coworkers at Starbucks, aware of what's new on television and in the theaters. We stay current with popular culture—the trendsetters, the movers and shakers, the media idols of our age.

But they are not teaching us how to live life. Not even close. Most of what takes up the airwaves is the absence of life—a constant reshuffling of relationships, a preoccupation with wiping out the opposition as violently as possible, the pursuit and spending of the almighty dollar in a system that Vaclav Havel calls "totalitarian consumerism." We see example after example of empty, self-centered existence.

We also don't know how to teach our kids about living life. We expect them to figure it out on their own, to sort of fall into it. We expect them to learn life from their peers.

If we are going to recover real life—the life that has been sucked out of us by technological gadgetry, vivid media images, and our

13

passive kind of continuing education via sitcoms and advertising—we are going to have to return to the wisdom of the ancients.

The key to living life is paradox. One of the most important paradoxes comes from the mouth of Jesus: "For whoever wants to save his life will lose it, but whoever loses his life for me will find it" (Matthew 16:25). That's a mouthful. Our aim in this book is to unpack the paradoxes for living true life and to begin to get good at it. If we do, we will also influence our kids. They will pick up a different set of values than what comes at them five hours a day over the tube.

Real life does not come naturally. It is counterintuitive. It is a skill we have to learn. That's because the way to real life is not something we get, but something we give. And here is another paradox: We can't get the life we want by direct effort. We will need to learn spiritual disciplines that are, in the words of Dallas Willard, "activities that are in our power that enable us to do what we cannot do by direct effort."[1] That's another mouthful—but that's what Klaus and I want to unpack in this book.

THE PURSUIT OF HAPPINESS

Do you want to be happy? If you are an American, it is overwhelmingly likely that you do. We Americans are obsessed with being happy. But we are also terribly confused about what happiness is. As a result, we seldom find a happiness that lasts. But because "the pursuit of happiness" is promised to us as a right in the founding document of our nation, the Declaration of Independence, we carry a sense of entitlement. We think we deserve happiness. And if we don't find what we consider to be happiness, we are likely to develop what the French demographer of early America, Alexis de Tocqueville, called "a strange melancholy in the midst of abundance."[2]

Our understanding of happiness has not always been so confused. Since the time of the ancients (the Greek philosophers Plato and Aristotle, and the Hebrew figures Moses and Solomon), right up through the church fathers (such as Augustine), and on through the Reformation, until around the 1700s in Britain—almost everyone agreed about what happiness was. When the Declaration of Independence says we have a right to the pursuit of happiness, the authors meant what almost everyone had meant prior to that time.

The Founding Fathers looked to the eighteenth-century English jurist William Blackstone for wisdom about where happiness comes from. He wrote, "[The Creator] has so intimately connected, so inseparably woven, the laws of eternal justice with the happiness of each individual, that the latter cannot be attained but by observing the former; and if the former be punctually obeyed, it can not but induce the latter."[3] Though Blackstone's language is archaic, he meant the same thing that C. S. Lewis intended when he wrote, "You can't get second things by putting them first; you can get second things only by putting first things first."[4] Or as Jesus said, "Seek first his kingdom and his righteousness, and all these things will be given to you as well" (Matthew 6:33).

We will look more closely at what the earlier writers meant by *happiness* in a moment. But first let's think about what has happened in the past hundred years or so, because the shift in meaning is destroying people's lives.

A recent dictionary definition of happiness is "a sense of pleasurable satisfaction."[5] Notice that happiness is identified with a feeling and, more specifically, a feeling very close to pleasure. Today the good life is a life of good feeling, and that is the goal of most people for themselves and their children. A major talk-radio host has interviewed hundreds of people over the past few years by asking the question "What did your parents want most for you—success, wealth, to be a good person, or happiness?" Eighty-five percent said happiness.

When my daughter's eighth-grade team was being creamed in a soccer game, the coach said at halftime, "Girls, don't worry about the score. The reason we play soccer is to have fun; so let's try to have a blast during the second half and go home happy whatever the final result." That coach reminds me of Cyndi Lauper's song "Girls Just Wanna Have Fun." He was mindlessly parroting the cultural mantra that pleasurable satisfaction is the goal of life. The reasons my wife and I wanted our daughter to play soccer were to learn how to win and to lose, to cooperate with others, to sacrifice for a long-term goal, which requires delaying instant gratification, and—well, you get the picture. What was really sad was not simply the coach's speech, but the fact that none of the parents so much as batted an eye at his counsel.

So what, you may be asking, is so wrong with happiness understood as a sense of pleasurable satisfaction or fun? In one sense, nothing. All things being equal, I would rather have fun than not have fun. But in another sense, everything. There are two main problems with this understanding. First, it represents a serious departure from a more ageless definition. When the classical understanding is clarified, as I will attempt in the next section, pleasurable satisfaction is exposed as inferior in value to happiness by its classical definition.

In a consumer culture, advertisers have a vested interest in creating in us a constant sense of dissatisfaction so we will buy products to regain happiness and satisfaction. This makes life a roller coaster and creates an insatiable need to be filled with pleasure. It creates too much pressure for anyone to bear. Among other things, it implies that the hard virtues of discipline, sacrifice, and their kin are intrinsically evil.

Further, happiness cannot be obtained by seeking it according to the contemporary sense of the word. If you have ever tried to be happy, you know this is true. Pleasurable satisfaction makes a very poor lifetime goal; it is, however, a wonderful by-product of striving after happiness in the classical sense. Think about it. If happiness is having an internal feeling of fun or pleasurable satisfaction, and if it is our main goal, where will we place our focus all day long? The focus will be on us, and the result will be a culture of self-absorbed individuals who can't live for something larger than we are. As parents, we will then view our children as a means to our own happiness. Marriage, work, and even God himself will exist as a means to making us happy. The entire universe will revolve around our internal pleasure—me!

What I am saying is no mere theoretical assertion. Since the 1960s, for the first time in history a culture—ours—has been filled with what have been called empty selves. The empty self is now an epidemic in America (and in much of Western cultures). According to Philip Cushman, "The empty self is filled up with consumer goods, calories, experiences, politicians, romantic partners, and empathetic therapists. . . . [The empty self] experiences a significant absence of community, tradition, and shared meaning, . . . a lack of personal conviction and worth, and it embodies the absences as a chronic, undifferentiated emotional hunger."[6] Popular teenage culture provides a clear example of a social system that produces and contains an abundance of empty selves. Sadly, the traits of the empty self do not leave at the age of twenty; studies show that they continue until around forty and, increasingly, last longer than that.

The empty self has a set of values, motives, and habits of thought, feeling, and behavior that make progress in maturity in the Way of Christ extremely difficult. Following are four traits of the empty self that undermine intellectual growth and spiritual development. As you read them, keep in mind that these result from redefining happiness as pleasurable satisfaction and making it the main, long-term goal of life.[7] Perhaps you'll be able to recognize some of these characteristics in people you come into contact with. (You might even see a few reflected in your own life.) As you note these traits, see if you agree about how harmful they are.

1. The empty self is inordinately individualistic. A few years ago, I was sitting in an elementary school gym with other parents at a D.A.R.E. graduation (a public school program designed to help children "say no to drugs") for my daughter's sixth-grade class. Five sixth graders were about to read brief papers expressing their reasons for why they would say no to drugs. As it turned out, each paper was a variation of one reason for refusing to take drugs: self-interest. Student after student said that he or she would refuse drugs because of a desire to stay healthy, become a doctor or athlete, or do well in school.

Conspicuous by its absence was the moral factor: not a single reference to duty to community or virtue before God. Not one student said that drugs were anathema because of the shame it would bring to family, community, or God. Individualistic reasons were the only ones given. By contrast, when a Japanese ice skater fell during an Olympic performance years ago, her main concern was not the endorsement opportunities she had lost. She felt bad for her family and the people who supported her so faithfully. Community loomed large in the way she understood her own self.

A healthy form of individualism is a good thing. But the empty self that populates American culture is a self-contained individual who defines his own life goals, values, and interests as though he were a human atom, isolated from others with little need or responsibility to live for the concerns of his broader community. The self-contained individual does his own thing and seeks to create meaning by looking within his own self. But as psychologist Martin Seligman warns, "The self is a very poor site for finding meaning."[8]

2. The empty self is infantile. It is widely recognized that adolescent personality traits are staying with people longer today than in earlier generations, sometimes continuing to manifest themselves into the late thirties. Created by a culture filled with pop psychology, schools, and media that usurp parental authority, and television ads that seem to treat everyone as a teenager, the infantile part of the empty self needs instant gratification, comfort, and soothing. The infantile person is controlled by cravings and constantly seeks to be filled with and made whole by food, entertainment, and consumer goods. Such a person is preoccupied with sex, physical appearance, and body image. He or she tends to live by feelings and experiences.

For the infantile personality type, pain, endurance, hard work, and delayed gratification are anathema. Pleasure is all that matters, and it had better be immediate. Boredom is the greatest evil; amusement, the greatest good.

3. *The empty self is narcissistic.* Narcissism is an inordinate and exclusive sense of self-infatuation in which the individual is preoccupied with his or her self-interest and personal fulfillment.[9] Narcissists manipulate relationships with others (including God) to validate their self-esteem, and they cannot sustain deep attachments or make personal commitments to something larger than ego. The narcissist is superficial and aloof, and prefers to "play it cool" and "keep my options open." Self-denial is out of the question.

The Christian narcissist brings a Copernican revolution to the Christian faith. Historically, Copernicus dethroned the earth from the center of the universe and put the sun in its place. Spiritually, the narcissist dethrones God and His purposes in history from the center of the religious life and places his or her personal fulfillment in the middle. The Christian narcissist evaluates the local church, books, and religious practices based on how they will further his or her agenda. The church becomes a means of fulfilling personal needs. God becomes another tool in a bag of tricks, along with the narcissist's car, workouts at the fitness center, and so on, which exist as mere instruments to facilitate a life defined independently of a biblical worldview.

The narcissist sees education solely as a means to the enhancement of his or her career. The humanities and general education, which historically were part of a university curriculum to help develop people with the intellectual and moral virtues necessary for a life directed at the common good, just don't fit into the narcissist's plans. As Christopher Lasch notes, "[Narcissistic] students object to the introduction of requirements in general education because the work demands too much of them and seldom leads to lucrative employment."[10]

4. *The empty self is passive.* The couch potato is the role model for the empty self, and there can be no doubt that Americans are becoming increasingly passive in their approach to life. We let other people do our living and thinking for us: The pastor studies the Bible for us, the news media does our political thinking for us, and we let our favorite sports team exercise, struggle, and win for us. From watching television to listening to sermons, our primary agenda is to be amused and entertained. Holidays have become vacations. Historically, a holiday was a "holy day," an intrinsically valuable, special, active change of pace in which, through proactive play and recreation, you refreshed your soul. A vacation is a "vacating"—even the language is passive—in order to let someone else amuse you. The passive individual is a self in search of pleasure and consumer goods provided by others. Such an individual increasingly becomes a shriveled self with less and less ability to be proactive and take control of life.

When people live for pleasurable satisfaction, they become empty selves and, because God did not make us to live for "happiness," our lives fall apart. Seligman has spent his career studying happiness.[11] In the late 1980s, he noted that with the baby boom generation, Americans experienced a tenfold increase in depression compared to earlier generations.[12] If any condition increases this much in the span of one generation, we are safe to say an epidemic has occurred.

A cause and cure must be sought. To our knowledge, Seligman is not a Christian, but his insights read as if they came from Holy Scripture. He claimed that the cause of this epidemic was the fact that baby boomers stopped imitating their ancestors and seeking daily to live for a cause bigger than they—God, family, one's country—and instead spent from morning to night trying to live for themselves and their own pleasurable satisfaction. It is clear that such a strategy brings depression, not pleasure—or much else.

In 2001, Hollywood publicist Michael Levine wrote a cover article in *Psychology Today* in which he argued that constant exposure to beautiful women has made men less interested in dating (if single) or in their wives (if married).[13] Levine cited studies in which men were exposed to (nonpornographic) pictures of beautiful actresses. The men were then asked to rate the desirability of a typical woman in their social environment (if single) or of their wives. In both cases they were much less interested in the women available to them. Levine pointed out that for all of human history prior to the automobile and television, the average man was exposed to very few people in general and to very few extremely beautiful women in particular. Limited in travel and with no television, most men learned to relate to women on a basis other than beauty. But today, said Levine, the average man sees plenty of absolutely gorgeous women each night on television shows and commercials and gradually loses interest in the women in his "real life."

These findings are not hard to believe. What is surprising, and relevant to our discussion, is Levine's explanation for this loss of interest. It is not that such exposure to television makes men think their partners are less physically attractive. Instead, men think,

"My partner is fine, but why settle for fine when there are so many beautiful women out there? I can do a lot better than this!"

This is the deepest insight Levine offers, but we offer one deeper still. Why is it that men think this way? Answer: They are empty selves, drunk with seeking happiness and, as a result, individualistic, narcissistic, infantile people who approach others as objects that exist merely to make them happy. Slowly but surely, the contemporary notion of happiness is killing our relationships, our religious fervor, our very lives.

The current understanding of happiness identifies it as a pleasurable feeling. Pleasant feelings are surely better than unpleasant ones, but the problem today is that people are obsessively concerned with feeling happiness; people are slaves to their feelings. Feelings are wonderful servants but terrible masters. When people make happiness their goal, they do not find it and, as a result, start living their lives vicariously through identification with celebrities.

People literally need to get a life. They need to find something bigger and more important to live for than pleasurable satisfaction, and they need to find a new strategy for daily life besides self-absorption. Contemporary psychologists are coming to agree about this, but we Christians did not need to wait for the latest word from science to know it. The Founder of our way of life actually put His finger on an alternative quite a few years ago.

GENUINE HAPPINESS AND HOW TO GET IT

According to the historical record of Jesus' deeds and teachings, there was one incident in His adult life that may have been a turning point, a climax in His public activities, second only to His execution, resurrection, and ascension. This incident occurred at a time when Jesus made clear to those to whom He would entrust His mission exactly who He was and what lay before Him.

Of paramount importance for raising children, being a good father or mother, learning to be a good boss or employee, or simply flourishing as a human, is Jesus' selection of topics to address immediately after making His identity clear. Clearly, the timing of what He taught indicates how central the teaching itself is. Here are His own words:

> "If anyone wishes to come after Me, he must deny himself, and take up his cross and follow Me. For whoever wishes to save his life will lose it; but whoever loses his life for My sake will find it. For what will it profit a man if he gains the whole world and forfeits his soul? Or what will a man give in exchange for his soul?" (Matthew 16:24-26, NASB)

It is critically important to grasp the core of what Jesus is saying. A mistake at this point could lead—no, has led many—to adopt a life strategy that has harmed them greatly. For example, people have taken Jesus to be affirming the idea of justification by works or a gruesome form of self-hatred. In context, Jesus is actually expressing a crucial insight about the nature of the gospel He brought. That gospel is often confused with being merely what some call "a gospel of sin management." This gospel is the message of justification by faith: that by being murdered on the cross, Jesus paid the penalty for our sins, that His righteousness is credited to those who trust what He did for them, and that in this act they cease to be separated from God and are, instead, headed for heaven when they die. The message of forgiveness of sins is a treasure in itself, an absolutely central part of the gospel, the emotional and spiritual impact of which was wonderfully captured by Mel Gibson's movie *The Passion of the Christ.*

While forgiveness is an important part of the gospel, the good news goes beyond that. It amounts to the claim that the kingdom of God—the direct availability of God himself and His rule—is now available to anyone who will enter it through trust in Jesus. And such an entrance provides the believer with the power and resources to learn how to live a radically new kind of life from above—approximating the life Jesus himself lived, a life that radically and progressively manifests the fruit of God's Spirit (see Galatians 5:22-23). The gospel is an invitation to new life in the kingdom, lived from the power of the indwelling Spirit and the resurrection power of Jesus himself. Properly understood, it is an invitation to a life of happiness obtained in a very specific way.

Here we must examine the classical understanding of happiness proclaimed by Moses, Solomon, Jesus, Aristotle, Plato, the church fathers and medieval theologians, and many more—the understanding that has recently been replaced by "pleasurable satisfaction." According to the ancients, happiness is *a life well lived, a life of virtue and character, a life that manifests wisdom, kindness, and goodness.*[14] For them, the life of happiness—the life to dream and fantasize about, to hunger and seek after, to imitate and practice—is a life of virtue and character. At its core, such a life includes a very deep sense of well-being. But this sense should not be confused with pleasurable satisfaction. The following chart may help clarify the difference.

CONTRASTING VIEWS OF HAPPINESS

Contemporary Happiness: Pleasurable satisfaction	*Classical Happiness:* Virtue and well-being
1. An intense feeling	1. A settled tone
2. Dependent on external circumstances	2. Springs from within
3. Transitory and fleeting	3. More permanent and stable
4. Addictive and enslaving	4. Empowering and liberating
5. Split off from rest of self, doesn't color rest of life, creates false/empty self	5. Integrated with entire personality, colors everything else, creates true self
6. *Strategy:* Achieved by self-absorbed narcissism	6. *Strategy:* Achieved by self-denying apprenticeship to Jesus
Outcome: Success produces a celebrity	*Outcome:* Success produces a hero

This chart contrasts five characteristics of each view of happiness, and the final row compares two diametrically opposed strategies for obtaining happiness—along with two very different results of those strategies. Let's begin by examining these characteristics.

An intense feeling is a vivid state. Rage, exuberance, and horror are intense feelings, as is pleasurable satisfaction. A settled tone, such as having a sense of being a wise or kind person, does have a felt texture to it, but it is subtler than an intense feeling. A settled tone is more like soft background music, which is not the direct object of one's awareness but rather the thing that creates an overall mood or texture. For instance, when at a restaurant, a man may be focusing his attention on his wife's statements and not on the background music. Still, that music can set the tone for the entire evening. When a person has an intense feeling, it is the focus of his attention. By contrast, if a person has a feeling that feels like a settled tone, it is subtler than an intense feeling, but, like background music, the feeling can set the tone for one's life.

Pleasurable satisfaction is heavily dependent on external circumstances (for example, performing well in a game or even at church, or enjoying a movie). As such, it is relatively unstable and comes and goes with the flux of a person's circumstances. Classical virtue springs from within as a process of maturation shapes internal character. Classical happiness becomes increasingly stable, permanent, and tied to a life of goodness, truth, beauty, and discipleship. It has less and less to do with external circumstances.

Like Turkish Delight in *The Lion, the Witch and the Wardrobe*, contemporary happiness becomes addictive and enslaving if it is central to the sense of self. Such an overemphasis creates a person who cannot live without "happiness," who lives an adrenalized life, whose empty self must constantly be filled with calories, romance, consumer goods, and social status. In this way, "happiness" becomes addictive and enslaving. Satisfaction of desire and the right to do what he or she wants are the goal of life. Classical happiness is deeply liberating to such a person, as he or she increasingly becomes a unified person who lives for a cause larger than self. Advancing the kingdom of God, living in intimacy with God and others, and honoring God by reflecting His good nature are the goals of life. People with these goals seek the power to live as they ought and are not preoccupied with the right to do what they want.

People who consume large chunks of "happiness" can live strangely compartmentalized lives. A pocket of happiness in their mind can be entirely split off from the rest of their life. For example, a sports fan can get a bit of "happiness" by watching a game, but after it wears off, the impact of being "happy" does not necessarily make him or her satisfied with marriage or work. By contrast, a life of virtue and its deep sense of well-being colors everything, because it forms the core of the self and becomes the integrative center around which all aspects of his or her life are unified.

The difference between the two senses of happiness should be clear. However, for the Christian the question arises: Is classical happiness really what Jesus is talking about in Matthew 16:24-26 (the passage we looked at earlier)? I believe it is, and that Jesus and other New Testament writers give it a distinctive texture. Jesus is not talking about going to heaven and not hell, nor is He teaching His followers how to avoid a premature death. Matthew included this line: "What will it profit a man if he gains the whole world and forfeits his soul?" (verse 26, NASB). Luke clarified Jesus' meaning of *soul* by simply using the word *himself*. The idea is finding self versus losing self. More specifically, to find your self is to find out what life should look like and to learn to live that way. It is to become like Jesus himself and have a character that manifests the radical nature of the kingdom of God and the fruit of the Spirit. It is to find out God's purposes for your life and to fulfill those purposes in a Christ-honoring way.

Remember, the concept of eternal life in the New Testament is not primarily one of living forever in heaven, but of having a new *kind* of life now. This new kind of life is so different that those without it can be called dead, truly. This is a life of human flourishing; a life lived the way we were made to function; a life of virtue, character, and well-being lived like and for the Lord Jesus.

This is what people hunger for, whether they know it or not. We are created for drama. We are meant to live dramatic lives as part of a worldwide movement—a divine conspiracy to trample the forces of darkness and replace them with goodness, truth, and beauty. Such a dramatic calling makes the presence or absence of a fleeting amount of pleasurable satisfaction simply beside the point and, frankly, not worth worrying about. We love movies that feature drama because that is how our own lives should be lived. We are to be dramatic even in the "little" things that grace the daily routines of our "ordinary" lives. As part of a pursuit of classical happiness, little things and ordinary activities become big and extraordinary pretty quickly.

No wonder people who are preoccupied with pleasurable happiness become empty selves. Their vision is too small, too confining, too mundane to justify their fourscore and ten, too little to demand their best effort over the long haul. Given the emptiness of such a perspective, when the gospel breaks into their hearts, it is no wonder people would rather spend themselves for an important cause—specifically, the cause of Christ and leading a life well lived—than enjoy a pampered idleness. They are weary of being flatlined by pleasure seeking. No wonder the primary problem of contemporary culture is boredom.

In this passage in Matthew, self-denial does not mean living without money, goods, recognition, or pleasurable satisfaction, though it certainly implies that having these things should not be your life objective. Neither is self-denial the attitude of putting yourself down. I sometimes meet people who cannot take a compliment. Or they feel guilty because they receive satisfaction from an achievement or from driving a new car or from some other earthly pleasure. Later we will correct this confusion about biblical happiness. For now, we note that Jesus uses taking up a cross to characterize self-denial. Luke added the word *daily* to the admonition (9:23), so it is apparent Jesus did not mean this literally, for we cannot die on a cross every day (though a willingness to die is clearly implied). Taking up our cross daily means to form the habit of going through our day with a certain orientation and attitude, namely, with a passion to give up our right to make ourselves the center of concern that day. Rather we live for God's kingdom, finding our place in His unfolding plan and playing our role well as we give our life away to others for Christ's sake.

The final row in the previous chart presents two very different approaches to life, producing two radically different types of people.

It is here that the two understandings grab us by the nape of the neck, shake us to the core, and demand we make a choice of lifestyle strategies. This choice is as important as any we will ever make. And that is not religious hype—it is the sober truth.

If pleasurable satisfaction is our goal, then day by day, from morning to night, we will be looking inside ourselves, constantly taking our own happiness temperature. Our activities (job, recreation, church involvement) and other people (friends, spouse, children, and even God) will be mere things, mere objects that simply exist as means to our own happiness. If we become self-absorbed, we often will withdraw from people. Of course, solitude for the right reasons is crucial. We seek solitude in part so that we may reenter relationships with solid boundaries and emotional/ spiritual refreshment. But if our pursuit is self-centered, we will resist and perhaps even attack others. We will look for safety that keeps us from having to change. If we are outgoing, on the other hand, we might talk all the time in social situations and not develop the skills of a good listener. And if we do know how to listen to others, it will be a front to earn the right to turn the conversation back to us at the earliest opportunity. After several years of this sort of life, we will become empty narcissists. This sounds harsh, but it is the truth—it's too important for sugarcoating.

If character and deep well-being is our goal, we will learn to see ourselves in light of a larger cause: the outworking of God's plan in history. We will be preoccupied with finding our role in that cause and playing it well. Our passion will be to see all of life's activities as occasions to draw near to—and become like—the triune God. We will hunger to become the kind of person who skillfully makes those around us better at living their lives as well. Our long-term focus will be on giving ourselves away to others for Christ's sake.

If we want to become people who flourish in life, with a deep sense of well-being, we must learn to give our lives away. As secular scholar John W. Gardner acknowledges, "Existence is a strange bargain. Life owes us little; we owe it everything. The only true happiness comes from squandering ourselves for a purpose."[15] As followers of Jesus, if we want to flourish as persons, we must give ourselves away for Christ's sake.

At this point, we need to correct some potential misunderstandings:

Are you saying that pleasurable satisfaction is bad? Absolutely not! We are saying three things. First, pleasurable satisfaction is a good thing, but there are other types of satisfaction that are more important (for example, becoming a wise, kind person). Second, in general, pleasurable satisfaction is a poor long-term goal, but an excellent by-product of the correct life goal (becoming like Jesus). Think about it. The paradox of contemporary happiness is that the more we try to get it, the less of it we have. The best way to be happy in the contemporary sense is to basically forget about it and focus on living for Christ and becoming a good person. We will gain more pleasure doing that than we will if we make pleasure itself a long-term goal. Third, pleasurable satisfaction is an appropriate short-term goal. We all need times when we watch television, go to a movie, take a vacation, and so forth. In these regular activities, we should, indeed, make our aim that of being happy. That's because happiness is a very good thing; it's just not important enough to justify our life on this earth.

Are you saying that I need to be harsh with myself and learn to get rid of self-love, that I need to be a doormat that simply serves others with no thought to my own well-being? Absolutely not! For one thing, to become like Christ we need to be disciplined but not self-loathing. We need to learn to be gentle with ourselves so we have what it takes to travel this road for the duration of life. To be gentle with something, we need to see it as simultaneously precious and vulnerable. This is why we are gentle with puppies. To be gentle with ourselves, we need to see ourselves as precious persons who are vulnerable and needy.

For example, if we are going through a time of serious anxiety and depression, though while we still seek to focus on others as best we can, it is also a time for us to be extremely gentle with ourselves and do what it takes to get well. And whether or not we are going through deep waters, we can lead a skillfully lived life only if we can draw appropriate boundaries and not let ourselves be inappropriately used over the long haul. Of course, there may be times when we allow someone to use us, but those times are appropriate only if they include wisely chosen boundaries that we freely draw.

Do I need to hide my problems from others to gain virtue and well-being so my issues don't get in the way? Again, absolutely not! A lifestyle of hiding from others is not a virtuous life. It deeply hinders the maturation process. As Henri Nouwen reminds us, "Laying down your life means making your own faith and doubt, hope and despair, joy and sadness, courage and fear available to others as ways of getting in touch with the Lord of life."[16]

Jesus' teaching is not bad news—it's the very nectar of life. If we are dominated by the quest for pleasurable satisfaction, we will not experience a flourishing life. But if we learn to give our life away for Christ's sake, we will find pleasurable satisfaction as well—but we will not be discouraged if it comes and goes. We will have bigger fish to fry.

Still, a major problem continues to plague our discussion: How do we learn to deny ourselves for Jesus' sake? We'll tackle that question in the next chapter.

QUESTIONS FOR PERSONAL REFLECTION
OR GROUP DISCUSSION

1. What would you say is the most common understanding of *happiness* today? For example, what comes across as happiness on television? What does happiness mean to the people you know at work? At school?

2. Does a particular character on television, in a movie, or in a book come to mind who depicts many of the characteristics of the empty self? Why? What's the problem with being an empty self?

3. Read the passage discussed in this chapter, Matthew 16:24-26. How have you tended to understand this passage? Do any of the insights from the author change what you hear Jesus teaching in this passage?

4. After just reading this first chapter, how do you think it's possible to take up your cross daily and still enjoy life? What is the author trying to say to Christians about living with the paradoxes of life?

CHAPTER TWO

GAINING HAPPINESS
BY LOSING YOUR LIFE

THE GOSPEL OF THE KINGDOM OF GOD—THESE ARE NOT EMPTY words; they are shorthand for a revolution. The gospel of the kingdom is an invitation to a different reality, a different way of living. The kingdom is a new way of relating as people. Where ordinary human life is based on competitiveness and defensiveness, domination and subjugation, treachery and violence, the kingdom is based on the self-giving love of God. This kingdom grows from the seed that falls to the ground and dies—it grows to new life from the death of Christ, which is God's love exhibited to us in its most brilliant glory (see John 12:23-24).

The kingdom brings liberation instead of confinement, celebration instead of despair, a crown of beauty instead of the ashes of mourning. It brings solace to the brokenhearted and the good news of hope for the poor (see Isaiah 61:1-3). The kingdom is a life of flourishing (see John 10:10), an experience of the ongoing presence of a tender, protecting Father, along with His Son and Spirit (see John 17). It means a life of love, peace, self-control, and virtue (see Galatians 5:22-23).

In short, the kingdom is a vision worth dying for. It is a life worth fighting for—against the vision of a world of isolated, self-centered, and empty selves, all vying for prominence and grasping for what they feel life owes them.

THE GLORIOUS VISION

In the first chapter, we looked at how true happiness—as defined by the ancients—is vastly different from the popular version of today. We spoke of self-denial. Now we must see that the only way to receive the kingdom of God is through the daily discipline of following Christ. This is a call to a higher life, a life that will require a commitment of all our strength (see Luke 10:27), and yet we will have sufficient grace to help us, because Jesus places on us His easy yoke (see Matthew 11:29).

The path of self-denial makes room for God in our lives. John W. Frye writes, "What is a spiritual discipline? It is simply a human activity that creates a space or setting for God to work."[1] Our aim is to allow God in His power to creatively and redemptively respond to situations that occur in our lives. This requires us to learn how to retreat from the usual flooding of our senses with the world and then to reengage in godly ways wherever He leads us.

Each of us can identify a few people who have made noticeable progress in living the reality of the kingdom. But we have to admit that this sort of life does not pervade our churches, and those who reach maturity seem to be rare. But on pain of discouragement, we dare not let the current condition of the Western church establish for us the possibilities of our own spiritual growth. Throughout the history of the Christian faith, and currently in various parts of the world as well as occasionally in our fellowships, there is a steady development of vibrant Christians who out-live, out-think, and out-die those who practice a rival religion or ideology. But unfortunately, these examples are uncommon.

What is wrong with the church today? I (J. P.) don't believe we lift our eyes high enough. I don't believe we see the magnificence of the Lord of Scripture, the glory of His work on the Cross, or the beauty of human relationships He has founded on the relational wealth of His kingdom.

Let me make what may seem to be an unusual statement: *Christianity is an aesthetic religion (a faithful pursuit of the glory of God) whose transforming power is tapped by regular and rigorous discipline and self-denial, done in constant dependence on the filling and power of the Holy Spirit.* Our purpose in the chapters that follow will be to unpack this statement and make our findings—specifically the transforming practice of the spiritual disciplines—our rule of life.

Happily, the spiritual disciplines are being reintroduced to the Western church, though they are still the object of much confusion and neglect. It is still rare to find a church that has a strategy for incorporating them into its mission statement and church calendar. In this chapter, we will explain what spiritual disciplines are and how they work, and we hope to fill your heart with a hunger to enter into them. Let's begin with the basics.

LEARNING TO PLAY GOLF AND PIANO

We know what it means to learn a particular skill, such as playing golf or piano. Consider golf: We start by becoming motivated to learn, then by reading about how to play or perhaps by watching a golf video. But where does the real learning come in? Practice. And more practice. Then the cultivation of a practice of practice. The really great players are those who keep practicing regularly over the entire course of their career. To learn golf, we go to a golf instructor at a driving range, and, focusing on specific movements under the instructor's direction, we repeat those movements over and over again until habits are formed. We do the same thing in learning how to play the piano, speak French, make pottery, or learn math. Sometimes we repeat a practice exercise that is not enjoyable in itself but is merely a means to getting good at the craft. One practices piano scales, not to get good at the scales but to get good at playing complex musical pieces.

So far, so good. But what does this have to do with gaining our life and flourishing as followers of the Lord Jesus? A failure to answer that question—indeed, a failure even to ask it—has resulted in disaster for the church and countless disappointed, powerless Christians. The sad thing is that we know what to do to learn golf or some other activity, but we don't know the relevance of this for getting good at life as a whole. Long ago, Plato (428–348 BC) wisely noted, "There is no question which a man of any sense could take more seriously than . . . what kind of life one should live."[2] Elsewhere Plato observed that it would be a tragedy if a person could be content with life by having good health, wealth, great looks, and a lot of ease and pleasure, while at the same time not giving a moment's thought to the cultivation of skill at living life as a whole with virtue and character.[3]

A more profound thinker put the point quite succinctly: What good will it be for you to gain the whole world, yet forfeit your soul? Or what can you give in exchange for your soul? (see Matthew 16:26). Yet our culture is filled with folk who know how to become good at golf but not at being a great father, a wonderful wife, or more generally, a person who is just plain good at life itself. Even if they know what these things mean, often they are at a loss as to how to grow in them. So, what do learning to play golf or piano have to say to us about the spiritual life?

SPIRITUAL DISCIPLINES, SELF-DENIAL, AND GETTING GOOD AT LIFE

A number of New Testament texts seem a bit odd at first glance. It's hard to know how to take them if we do the right thing and interpret them literally. However, they are crucial to our aim of getting good at life. Please examine the following passages with me, especially the words I have italicized:

> Therefore I urge you, brethren, by the mercies of God, to present your *bodies* a living and holy sacrifice, acceptable to God, which is your spiritual service of worship. (Romans 12:1, NASB)

Romans 12:1 is unpacked earlier in Paul's letter as follows:

> Even so consider yourselves to be dead to sin, but alive to God in Christ Jesus. Therefore do not let sin reign in your mortal body so that you obey its lusts, and do not go on

presenting *the members of your body* to sin as instruments of unrighteousness; but present yourselves to God as those alive from the dead, and *your members* as instruments of righteousness to God. . . . I am speaking in human terms because of *the weakness of your flesh*. For just as you *presented your members* as slaves to impurity and to lawlessness, resulting in further lawlessness, so now *present your members* as slaves to righteousness, resulting in sanctification. (Romans 6:11-13,19, NASB)

Do you not know that those who run in a race all run, but only one receives the prize? Run in such a way that you may win. Everyone who competes in the games *exercises self-control* in all things. They then do it to receive a perishable wreath, but we an imperishable. Therefore I run in such a way, as not without aim; I box in such a way, as not beating the air; but I *discipline my body and make it my slave*, so that, after I have preached to others, I myself will not be disqualified. (1 Corinthians 9:24-27, NASB)

Therefore, *put to death the members of your body* to immorality, impurity, passion, evil desire, and greed. (Colossians 3:5, authors' paraphrase)

Discipline yourself for the purpose of godliness; for *bodily discipline* is only of little profit, but godliness is profitable for all things, since it holds promise for the present life and also for the life to come. (1 Timothy 4:7-8, NASB)

At first glance, these texts—especially the italicized words—can seem a bit puzzling. But, as we will discover, they express insights about human nature and flourishing so very deep that, once again, the insights of the Bible expose the shallowness of our culture in breathtaking fashion. To understand this biblical teaching, we must first clarify four concepts: *habit, character, flesh,* and *body.*

A *habit* is an ingrained tendency to act, think, or feel a certain way without needing to choose to do so. The way you write the letters of the alphabet is not something you need to think about. It is a habit learned years earlier, and you concentrate on what you are writing, not on the style of handwriting. *Character* is the sum total of your habits, good and bad. We could say that "penmanship character" is the sum total of your good and bad writing habits; it is your handwriting style.

Biblical terms such as *flesh* (*sarx* in the Greek) or *body* (*soma*) have a wide field of meaning, depending on the context. Sometimes *flesh* and *body* mean the same thing, but in the previous passages, there is a unique and important meaning for each. *Body* is pretty obvious. In contrast to the soul, it refers to our living, animated physical aspect. The body can be seen and touched, and it is composed of tissue, skin and bone, various organs (the heart, for example), and systems (the nervous system, for example).

Now, this is crucial: The *flesh* in these passages refers to the sinful tendencies or habits that reside in the body and whose nature is opposite that of the kingdom of God.[4] To understand these more fully and to appreciate their importance more deeply, let's return to learning to play golf. What I am about to say may sound a bit forced, but I mean for it to be taken literally.

When a man plays golf, he has a golf-character, that is, the sum of good and bad habits relevant for playing golf. His golf-flesh is the sum of his bad golf habits. Where do these bad habits reside? They dwell as ingrained tendencies in specific body parts, particular members of the body. His golf game may be weakened by bad habits in the wrists, the shoulders, or somewhere else. He may have good habits in his legs but bad habits, golf-flesh, residing in his shoulders. Golf-flesh resides in the specific members of his body.

How does he develop a good golf-character? Not simply by daily golf-readings coupled with regular exposure to motivational golf-music! No, he must present his members to a golf instructor at a driving range as instruments of golf "righteousness," instead of following his golf-flesh as an instrument of golf "unrighteousness." These are not figures of speech. Think of them as literal. By so presenting his members to a wise guide—a golf instructor—he can gradually get rid of bad golf-habits and replace them with good ones.

How does he present his members to a golf instructor? Two things are involved. First, he must dedicate himself to the pursuit of golf righteousness (to getting good at golf), and choose to submit as an apprentice to a master-teacher. Second, he does not simply engage in a one-time act of dedication to the master-teacher. To present his body to a golf instructor requires repeatedly engaging specific body parts in regular activities done over and over again, with the instructor in charge, and practicing different movements. For example, he may present the members of his body—say, the wrists—to the instructor by practicing over and over again a specific wrist movement, a particular swing. The result of such habitual bodily movement will be the replacement of bad habits that dwell in the wrists with good habits. The golf-flesh that resides in the wrists will give way to golf-righteousness in those members. Later the instructor may require the habitual presentation of other members—say, the hips—to replace bad habits that reside there.

A golf-discipline is a repeated golf exercise, a bodily movement involving specific body parts, repeated over and over again. This is done for the purpose of getting rid of golf-flesh and gaining golf-righteousness in the body. Notice that some golf-disciplines are done in practice in a way different from how they are done in the game. Like playing piano scales, they are performed to prepare the player for a different movement than actually takes place in the game. Like scales, the practice activity drops out during the real game (for example, an over-exaggerated swing to compensate for the tendency to hook the ball). Other practice activities are also done in the game (for example, keeping the head down while swinging). But the important thing is this: A golf-discipline is done repeatedly, not to get good at the discipline, but to get good at the game of golf.

THE DISCIPLINES OF ABSTINENCE
AND ENGAGEMENT

The parallels with becoming good at life should be clear. When we present our body to God as a living sacrifice (see Romans 12:1), this involves not just a one-time act of dedication, but a habitual, repeated bodily exercise (see 1 Timothy 4:7-8; 1 Corinthians 9:24-27) involving specific body parts (see Romans 6:12-13,19). This results in putting to death our bad habits (see Colossians 3:5), that is, removing the flesh that resides in those body parts and replacing it with righteousness that comes to reside in the members of our body. *A Christian spiritual discipline is a repeated bodily practice, done in dependence on the Holy Spirit and under the direction of Jesus and other wise teachers in His Way, to enable us to get good at certain things in life that we cannot learn to do by direct effort.*

In the same way that golf-flesh resides in specific body parts (for example, the wrists), so sinful habits often reside in specific body parts. For example, anger resides in the stomach area, anxiety in the chest or shoulders, gossip in the tongue and mouth region, and lust in the eyes and other areas. A spiritual discipline is a repetitive practice that targets one of these areas in order to replace bad habits with good ones in dependence on the Spirit of the living God. Some disciplines—for example, playing piano scales—have no value in themselves and are totally means to an end (in this case, learning to play beautiful music). You don't practice the piano for its own sake but to get good at playing the piano! Other disciplines, such as practicing being honest at golf, are not only valuable as means to an end when done on the driving range (they form the habit of telling yourself the truth, of being honest in character) but they are also intrinsically valuable for their own sake when done during the game itself (it is good in itself to be honest while playing a game of golf!).

In the same way, some spiritual disciplines, such as the practice of journaling (the habit of writing down prayers to God, daily experiences of answered prayer, good and bad events, and so forth), are mere means to an end. These might include learning to remember answers to prayer, learning to concentrate on incidental daily events as occasions that have spiritual significance, or learning to talk to God deliberately and with emotion. Other disciplines are both means to an end and intrinsically valuable skills in their own right when done during the actual "game" of life. In chapter 4, we will examine prayer. There we will explain how prayer is an example of a practice that is both intrinsically valuable and a means to an end.

Dallas Willard points out that there are two categories of spiritual disciplines: those of abstinence/detachment and those of engagement.[5] His list is not exhaustive, but it does contain most of the classical disciplines:

- Disciplines of abstinence: solitude, silence, fasting, frugality, chastity, secrecy, sacrifice
- Disciplines of engagement: study, worship, celebration, service, prayer, fellowship, confession, submission

In disciplines of abstinence, we unhook, detach, and abstain for a period of time and to varying degrees from the satisfaction of normal, appropriate desires, such as food, sleep, companionship, sex, music, comfort, financial security, recognition, and so forth. These disciplines help us address *sins of commission*—things we normally actively pursue. In general, it is not a good idea to detach from one of these without filling the resulting void with attachment to something positive. Therefore, disciplines of engagement go hand in hand with those of detachment. Engagement disciplines help us address *sins of omission*.

EXAMPLES OF TRAINING IN THE DISCIPLINES

In addition to classical examples of disciplines such as those already mentioned, any repeated practice that is fruitful for growth in Christlikeness is legitimately called a spiritual discipline, and thus the list of disciplines is endless. Here are two examples of "non-classical" disciplines.

The first is the discipline of witnessing. Several years ago, I (J. P.) debated one of the world's leading intellectual atheists in front of a packed auditorium at a university campus. The courage to do this came not only from depending on Christ in that moment, but also from the spiritual discipline of witnessing. Years earlier, I was scared to death to share my faith with anyone. What was I to do to become a calm, courageous witness for Christ? Of course, I read books on evangelism and tried to stay motivated through good music, worship, and fellowship with nurturing Christians. But if the thesis of this chapter is correct, then that would never have been enough. Transformation into a confident, skillful evangelist could come only if I practiced the discipline of witnessing over and over again.

I began with learning the contents of an evangelistic booklet. I also memorized my brief personal testimony, as well as a way to introduce myself to others and a way to excuse myself from conversation if needed. I practiced using the booklet and giving my testimony in front of the mirror repeatedly. Then I practiced my delivery over and over again with a Christian friend. Subsequently, I went witnessing about fifty times with someone more experienced. Gradually, I did more of the talking, until I was the one taking the experienced brother with me. Finally, I started taking novices myself and, eventually, I repeated a similar process for giving an evangelistic talk to crowds. By the time I debated the atheist in that auditorium, I had shared my faith hundreds of times. In all, I have participated in about twenty debates on different subjects, and although my ministry is now taking a different direction, I learned to evangelize by the spiritual discipline of repeated witnessing and testifying to my experience with Christ.

There is another discipline that, for lack of a better name, I'll call the discipline of smiling and projecting warmth to others. This is a critical spiritual discipline for those who see the glass half empty or who, for whatever reason, tend to be moody and shy in a way that blocks a vibrant testimony.

Attending a Sunday school class I taught on the disciplines was a young woman named Vicki. Vicki projected an unfriendly, sad personality, quite the opposite of warmth. When I talked to her about warmth and spiritual vitality, I was careful to distinguish it from having an outgoing personality. A vital, warm spiritual presence and outlook is something for which we should all strive, but personality types vary from person to person and are neither right nor wrong.

I told Vicki that I wanted her to practice smiling and speaking as warmly as she could to others throughout her day. I laid out a discipline of smiling in which she would practice smiling at herself each morning in the mirror, smiling at the first sight of a new face she would pass in the office or at the grocery store, and smiling at each half hour throughout the day. She was also to take the initiative in talking to others she met (socially, she was somewhat passive and hidden), look them in the eye, and say something warm to them (such as "your hair looks nice today" or "I hope you have a good weekend").

As I laid out this strategy, I explained to her that psychological studies have supported a biblical view of transformation: Attitudes can affect the body (for instance, worry can cause indigestion), but doing things with your body can also affect your attitudes. I assured her that if she would try this for a month, her outlook would become more positive, she would grow in her daily trust in God, and she would tend to focus more on others.

Initially, she objected to my strategy on the grounds that she would feel unnatural, even hypocritical, in doing this when she really didn't feel upbeat or warm toward others. I assured her of two things. First, nothing worth learning to do well—playing the piano or being warm and caring toward others—feels natural and easy to do in the early stages of forming the habit. That's just the way it is with habits. Second, I comforted her that it is not hypocritical to smile and be warm toward others even when you don't want to, as long as you *want* to want to. In other words, if she could sincerely say that being warm and friendly were traits she desired for herself, then wanting to want to be this way was sufficient for counting as sincerity in practicing these actions. Why? Because even though she didn't feel this way at the moment of expression, the fact that she really did want to develop this approach to life meant that she had permission from God and others to go through a learning process of forming these habits.

In one way or another, the rest of the book will weave relevant spiritual disciplines into the discussion. In the remainder of this chapter, we shall briefly examine a frequently associated pair of classical disciplines.

TWO FRIENDS: SOLITUDE AND SILENCE

The disciplines of solitude and silence are absolutely fundamental to the Christian life, and they are naturally practiced in tandem. In solitude we choose to be alone and to reflect on how we experience the facets of life (family, job, relationship with God, finances) and what they mean to us while in isolation. We unhook from companionship with others; we take ourselves physically and mentally out of our social, familial, and other human relationships.

We all have a false self—a person we tend to project that is not who we really are. The false self is a combination of social roles, others' expectations, our own strategies to be safe or to receive recognition, and our various inauthentic attachments to others and our environment (work, home, gym). The false self is enslaving and takes a lot of emotional and spiritual energy to sustain. It is a fragmented self, torn apart by the various competing voices that seek to shape it. The false self actually produces loneliness because—perhaps subconsciously—it reflects the belief that before one can be acceptable, one must put on a false identity and perform for others. The true self remains hidden and, therefore, lonely. Because we are often afraid of experiencing our thoughts and emotions, we become addicted to sounds (e.g., music, television). And soon, when we fill our lives with noise, it becomes difficult to be quiet enough to listen to what's going on inside of us or to God's still, small voice. Unfortunately, we cannot accurately hear others—God or loved ones—if we have not heard from ourselves.

Solitude is a way of breaking these attachments, even if briefly. By stepping outside the false self, we feel our true self in relationship to various aspects of our lives, especially in relationship to our distorted images of God. We can thereby learn how the false self has distorted those aspects. We are then in a better position to reenter our daily lives and make progress in becoming an authentic person. The true self that emerges from practicing isolation from others develops an inner solitude, a quality of being centered and quiet. Henri Nouwen put it this way:

> It is probably difficult, if not impossible, to move from loneliness to solitude without any form of withdrawal from a distracting world. . . . The solitude that really counts is the solitude of heart; it is an inner quality or attitude that does not depend on physical isolation. On occasion this isolation is necessary to develop this solitude of heart, but it would be sad if we considered this essential aspect of the spiritual life as a privilege of monks and hermits. It seems more important than ever to stress that solitude is one of the human capacities that can exist, be maintained and developed in the center of a big city, in the middle of a large crowd and in the context of a very active and productive life. A man or woman who has developed this solitude of heart is no longer pulled apart by the most divergent stimuli of the surrounding world but is able to perceive and understand this world from a quiet inner center.[6]

Because a person can learn to practice solitude in the anonymity of a crowd, silence is not necessary for practicing solitude, but it is a very useful aspect of it. Silence involves two things: First, a person closes off from sounds and seeks a quiet place. Second, he or she does not communicate with others.

How can we learn to practice solitude and silence? It is important to find activities that work for you. Realizing that there is no "thus saith the Lord" in this, we have found these ideas to be immensely helpful to our dear friends and to us.

First, remember that when you go into solitude and silence, your basic goal is to do nothing. Yes, nothing! You are to center yourself in quiet and rest. As you do that, you also focus on centering your affections on the Lord and His creation. This is not a time to catch up on your scheduled daily Bible reading or on anything else. In fact, if possible, the first thing you should do when engaging in solitude is to take off your watch.

Second, there are different occasions for entering solitude. Here are three suggestions:

1. Form the habit of practicing for an hour on two or three nights a week. After watching the evening news or before your favorite television program comes on (it is unrealistic to start by cutting off all television or all your ordinary habits—start modestly until a habit is formed), say from seven to eight o'clock, go to a favorite quiet place in your house or go for a walk. Some change of location, however small, is very helpful.

2. Practice driving in the slow lane with the radio and cell phone turned off. In all honesty, I have found that my commute to work (around thirty-five minutes one way) has been one of the most important places for my spiritual development in my weekly schedule. Practicing solitude while driving can make traffic a joy and your car a cathedral. Of special focus should be how you experience pressure from drivers who push you to go faster. We get in touch with how close to the surface our anger is, how easily we are manipulated by social pressure, and how quickly we project our feelings onto others. These insights are worth the price of admission, because one of the key benefits of solitude is that when we unhook from our support systems, our defective strategies for coping with life and our negative feelings that lie just beneath the surface manifest themselves. Then we have a chance to feel and think about them and invite Jesus to give wisdom and support in developing healthier habits and strategies.

3. *Once or twice a year, go alone on a solitude retreat* from 9 a.m. one day until 5 p.m. the next.[7] Go to a retreat center that has as one of its purposes the provision of a place for individual sojourners. Try to find a center that has gardens, fountains, statues, and other forms of beautiful artwork. In our experience, Catholic retreat centers are usually ideal for solitude retreats.

We recommend that you arrive at the center at about nine so you will have a full morning ahead of you yet won't have to get up so early that you are tired your first day. (By the way, if you need a nap on your retreat, by all means take one.) Take a Bible, notebook, and hymnal. But remember, a solitude retreat is not a time to catch up on reading; it is a time for quiet, reflection, and worship. We also recommend that you bring photos of your loved ones and a picture of Jesus. That way, your loved ones and the Lord Jesus can become steady objects of focus and love.

After checking in, stay in your room, get on your knees for around fifteen to thirty minutes, and dedicate the next thirty-two hours to God. When you kneel, be sure it is in a comfortable place. If you kneel at your bedside, open the Bible to a favorite passage, read it a few times, and pray it to Jesus. If you cannot kneel or walk, then sit or lie comfortably with the palms of your hands facing up, expressing to God that you are hungry to receive from Him. Then get up and go for a long, slow, quiet walk. If possible, walk where there are beautiful sounds and sights (for example, near fountains, flowers, a stream, or a beautiful statue).

As you quiet down, certain things will surface: anxious thoughts, worries about things you need to get done, tensions with work, family, or responsibilities. Don't fight them. If you fight against them, they will overwhelm you like an ocean wave, and you will become fixated on them. Just let them roll through your body, mind, and emotions. Pray about your concerns and, after a while, stop to look at a flower or to listen to a fountain. Or gaze at a statue of Jesus. Or let some pleasant thought, feeling, or memory run through your mind over and over again.

While focusing on some beautiful object or some pleasant memory, let joy and thanksgiving for the object or memory well up within you. Begin to sing a song to God. Take a passage you have memorized and that you dearly love and pray it over and over to God. Use this as an occasion to pause and give thanks for specific aspects of your life, from the wonderful taste of coffee to more important matters. As concerns spring up, talk again to Jesus about that. If you can't get worries off your mind, we suggest that you schedule time later on your first day, such as one hour before dinner, to do nothing but focus in prayer and meditation on your worries. That way, if a concern threatens to overwhelm you, you can tell yourself you will face it later.

After an hour or so, go back to your room and journal on whatever comes to your mind and heart. Then get back to praying, reading Scripture, singing, or meditating again for thirty minutes. When finished, sit in a comfortable chair and begin reading a book of the Bible. We recommend that you make it your goal to read an entire gospel during your retreat, not necessarily at one sitting. Read until you desire to stop, but be sure to pause repeatedly during your reading to pray, sing, or journal.

Move back and forth between (1) prayer and meditation on your knees (or with your palms facing up); (2) sitting (or lying) comfortably while journaling or reading Scripture; (3) walking (or viewing a pictorial book on nature) and pausing at beautiful sights that arrest your attention. This will form the staple of your entire solitude retreat. At various times, go into the chapel and worship. During the retreat, if it is not distracting, evaluate the past twelve to eighteen months of your life and set some modest goals for the next six months. Be sure to include some habit changes. Make the goals reasonable. And don't feel guilty if you get sleepy from time to time. Be sure to take naps if needed.

We also recommend that you don't fast on the retreat. Trying to combine fasting with solitude can be too difficult and joyless if you are not used to them. Take some snacks along to enjoy, but don't use them to fill your empty self. One purpose of the solitude retreat is to get in touch with that emptiness. Let snacking be a source of modest joy and an occasion for thankfulness for tastes; don't let it be a way of inordinately comforting or rewarding yourself.

Finally, remember that learning to do almost anything is hard in the early stages, and solitude and silence are no exception. But people trained in these disciplines develop boundaries, a sense of being centered, and an awareness of their true self so they can more healthily enter into mutually serving, loving relationships and more authentic labor as they live their daily life. Remember, Jesus himself frequently engaged in solitude and silence (see Mark 1:35; Luke 4:42). As His students in the school of life, it only makes sense that we follow Him in these activities.

In the early 1990s, newspapers across America carried a story with these words:

> A flurry of recent survey research has found that, contrary to the secularism of popular culture, Americans believe in God and identify themselves as strongly religious. But analysts who have studied the data say that the spirituality of many Americans might be only skin-deep. "Our biggest problem is not secular humanism, but interest in religion that doesn't turn into commitment in every day life," said Martin Marty, a prominent US church historian.[8]

Spiritual disciplines are practical means for learning how to grow in self-denial. Far from being bad news, the challenge to practice spiritual disciplines is good news. Disciplines are practices for gaining happiness. They are part of a heartfelt and thoughtful

Christian life preoccupied with the living God. In the next chapter, we begin to explore further the matters of the heart to encourage greater receptivity to God.

QUESTIONS FOR PERSONAL REFLECTION
OR GROUP DISCUSSION

1. Think about an activity or skill that you do well or have done well in the past (for example, participating in a sport, playing a musical instrument, speaking a foreign language, cooking, making home repairs, giving a presentation). Can you remember the steps you went through to become proficient at that skill?

2. The author notes that "a Christian spiritual discipline is a repeated bodily practice, done in dependence on the Holy Spirit and under the direction of Jesus and other wise teachers in His Way, to enable us to get good at certain things in life that we cannot learn to do by direct effort." Is there an area of spiritual discipline you would like to become more proficient in? Consider prayer, perhaps, or studying the Bible. What steps could you take to become good at this spiritual discipline?

3. Several Scripture passages were cited in this chapter regarding the importance of incorporating our body and its various members within the scope for growth toward Christian maturity. Which ones would you like to study or discuss further?

4. The author describes the two disciplines of solitude and silence. What would you like to try out in the next month?

CHAPTER THREE

FORMING A TENDER, RECEPTIVE HEART

THE SPIRITUAL LIFE IS A RELATED LIFE. WE ARE FUNDAMENTALLY related to God, but we are also bound in relationships with other human beings. And this is where some of our greatest struggles enter in. Relationships can be so difficult at times that we may agree with French existentialist Jean-Paul Sartre: "Hell is other people."[1]

And yet, if we are having problems in our relationships with others, we are certain to have trouble in our relationship with God. The apostle John wrote, "If anyone says, 'I love God,' yet hates his brother, he is a liar. For anyone who does not love his brother, whom he has seen, cannot love God, whom he has not seen" (1 John 4:20).

We will speak about forming friendships in the final chapter. However, now it is our task to look at our emotions, for within every one of our relationships, our emotions will always have a crucial part to play. Of course, this fact also applies to our relationship with God. If we desire to deepen our intimacy with God, we'll need to become more aware of how our emotional life affects our walk with Him. How we feel can move us either closer to God or further away. Emotions can also distort or clarify our view of God.

Our emotions can become a window for looking into the state of our soul. But if we're basically unaware of our feelings—as I (Klaus) was for most of my life—our emotional life actually becomes the hidden momentum and engine behind many of our actions. We *think* we're in the pilot seat of our life. But in reality, our dark emotions drive us forward unaware, and we do stupid and sinful things. Looking back over these mistakes and disasters of life, we wonder, "Why couldn't I see how dumb that was at the time?" The word *emotion* itself includes both the word and the idea of motion—emotions *move* us. So the more we can take notice of our emotional state, the more we can be guided by God and sustained by His grace to experience more of the abundant life Jesus promised.

Emotional activity is deeper than we often think, because there are two "kingdoms" vying for our allegiance, each wishing to reign in our heart: the kingdom of God and the dominion of Satan. Our emotional life is one important place where that battle rages. These supernatural forces powerfully affect how we feel. As Jesus said, "The thief [that is, Satan] comes only to steal and kill and destroy; I have come that they may have life, and have it to the full" (John 10:10). As we invite God into our emotional life, He will carry us and empower us by His goodness and grace.

YOU GOTTA HAVE HEART

In a word, I was clueless. It took an act of God while I was on a spiritual retreat to make me aware of the meaning of the deep churnings in my soul. Although I had been a believer for more than thirty years, I was unaware of the depths of my sinfulness before a holy God. And even though I had been a pastor and was then a seminary professor, I was still clueless. As God brought a deep-felt conviction to my heart of arrogance, self-righteousness, and pride, I sobbed for two hours straight.

How did God begin tenderizing this proud and stubborn heart? In my case, it didn't happen overnight. But over a six-year period, God slowly transformed a stoic, stubborn, and workaholic male into someone whose heart is now much more receptive to God, more open to hearing the truth about himself, and more ready to weep with those who weep.

My sins were most apparent in my relationship with my wife, Beth. One early evening at six, her brief comment— "Remember, I'll be needing the car at seven tonight"—suddenly stirred up my inner parts and brought about an energized outburst. I yelled, "You didn't bring this up when we were coordinating our schedules last Saturday!" Where was all that unexpected energy and irritation coming from? Why would I react so strongly to that comment? Various factors contributed to this surprising flare-up. I would have to rearrange my schedule and thus not make progress on an important project I was working on. Coupled with a few other similar setbacks earlier in the week unrelated to Beth's involvement, this schedule change had finally set me off.

My on-task drivenness was being checked. At one level I had erupted because of growing frustration. At another level, my "kingdom" had been invaded. All the coping strategies I'd learned in the past, mostly sinful, instantly and easily arose so I could self-righteously defend my fragile ego by blaming Beth for the problem. My response was really saying this: "This is your problem, not our problem. I'm in the right and you are in the wrong. Admit it; wilt before me and admit how wrong and sorry you are, which affirms my complete innocence. You will have to fix the problem by yourself. Rearrange your schedule, not mine. My kingdom's borders don't budge."

Pride, self-righteousness, selfishness, lack of love, lack of mercy. Her brief comment tapped the deep well of a deformed part of my soul. But I thought I was innocent. No, I was clueless. I was unaware of those ugly and unholy vices that clogged my spiritual veins, limiting God's work in me and through me. And it took an act of God to bring me to my knees and make me finally say "uncle."

At forty-six years of age I went on a three-week "guided" spiritual retreat of solitude. God showed up and performed open-heart surgery, uncovering these dark broodings of pride. On the retreat, I visited daily with a spiritual mentor for about an hour. The rest of the time was spent alone "wasting time" with God: praying, reading Scripture, singing, and journaling.[2]

During the third week, prompted to read Romans, I knelt at my bed and read chapter 1. When I got to verses 30 and 31, these words jumped out at me: *arrogant, boastful, unloving, unmerciful* (NASB). They became living and active words of conviction. Tenderly, yet forcefully, the God who is holy pierced my pride, exposing to me at a deep experiential level my desperate need for His mercy and continuing work in my life as a believer. This profound divine encounter continues to mark me as I am in the process of becoming more transparent, more merciful, more loving, and more humble — changes Beth affirms.

THAT ADDED EXTRA OF OUR EMOTIONS

Why do disagreements between mates or friends or coworkers always seem like wars? Why do we automatically take the posture of defending our turf at all costs? One moment we seem to be calm, cool, and collected. Then, all of a sudden, a volcano erupts, spewing destructive lava.

One day I was in a line of cars stopped at an intersection for a red light when the railroad crossing signal started sounding off. The long arm lowered across the road to prevent our way forward. I happened to look in my rearview mirror and noticed the man in the car directly behind me. He seemed to be engaged in an animated conversation with someone, but I didn't see anyone else in the car. Then I realized he wasn't very happy about waiting for the train to pass.

In the mirror, I was watching a man who was fully bursting with rage, yelling obscenities nonstop and at the top of his lungs, while the train passed by. He went from Silent Sam alone in his car to a raving madman in ten seconds flat. I chuckled—not at him, but at myself. Before my own acknowledgement of sin in this area, I would have been overwhelmed by feelings of contempt for the sinful performance behind me. But I had a new freedom to resist my arrogance and self-righteousness. I had become more aware of how sinful my own heart still is, so my chuckle was one of identification rather than of judgment.

By God's design, we are all *emotional* beings. The sooner we acknowledge this basic fact of life, the sooner we can make significant headway toward growing a tender heart that can listen to

God. This growth process may be especially difficult for us males in our Western culture, but even some women—Beth would include herself—need to learn more about experiencing a healthy and robust emotional life. In our culture, men can engage themselves with full emotional energy at the baseball park or in front of the football game on television or even while singing with gusto at church. But otherwise men are supposed to contain themselves, to be strong and silent. Weeping is for wimps.

Only late in life have I come to appreciate the importance of my emotions. In my particular branch of evangelicalism, we often use the so-called "train diagram" to emphasize the importance of believing in the factual truth of what the Bible teaches. The train diagram connects three key concepts together: fact, faith, and feeling. The engine represents fact, the coal car represents faith, and the caboose represents feeling. The main point of the illustration is that the train can run with or without feeling (the caboose), but facts and faith (the engine and the fuel) are essential; our faith in the biblical facts is the ground of identity as believers, regardless of how we feel about our relationship with God at any given time.

The underlying motivation of the analogy is commendable: to encourage those whose conversion experience and Christian life does not come with or evidence any particularly strong emotional responses. If you don't feel any different *after* responding to Jesus' call for His saving grace or during your subsequent walk with Him than you did *before* you became a Christian, that is acceptable. Yet the unintended effect of this teaching is to present a nonemotional model for conversion and Christian living that actually becomes the *norm* for how to live the Christian life. Too much emotion is suspect, so better tone down that side of your life because it really isn't all that important anyway. For most of my Christian life, I downplayed the legitimate role of emotions.

A BIBLICAL PATHWAY TO OUR HEART

We must look to Jesus to show us the way to be strong people who are compassionately tender at appropriate times. Jesus experienced a wide range of emotions himself. He openly wept (see John 11:35); He felt deep compassion for people (see Mark 6:34); He even displayed righteous anger (see Mark 3:5). And at one of the loneliest and most difficult times of His life, He confided with His close friends how horrible He felt and asked them to pray with Him:

> Then Jesus went with his disciples to a place called Gethsemane, and he said to them, "Sit here while I go over there and pray." He took Peter and the two sons of Zebedee along with him, and he began to be sorrowful and troubled. Then he said to them, "My soul is overwhelmed with sorrow to the point of death. Stay here and keep watch with me." (Matthew 26:36-38)

God also used Philippians 4:6-7 to open the gate for me to finally welcome feelings as an important part of my life before Him. There Paul wrote, "Do not be anxious about anything, but in everything, by prayer and petition, with thanksgiving, present your requests to

God. And the peace of God, which transcends all understanding, will guard your *hearts* and your *minds* in Christ Jesus" (emphasis added). Notice that if I'm not able to recognize the emotions of anxiety and worry, I won't be able to follow God's guidelines to seek Him, to share my concerns, and to receive His deep peace — another emotion.

Gerald Hawthorne explains that "this expression, 'the peace of God,' is found nowhere else in the NT. . . . Paul seems here to be referring to the tranquility of God's own eternal being, the peace of God which God himself has, the calm serenity that characterizes his very nature . . . which grateful, trusting Christians are welcome to share."[3] Furthermore, Hawthorne clarifies that although the term *kardia* (heart) in characteristic Hebrew fashion usually designates the whole person, a narrower focus is intended in this passage.

> But here, where Paul places *kardia* [heart] alongside *noema* [mind] grammatically in such a way as to distinguish the one from the other . . . *kardia* [heart] very likely has its meaning narrowed simply to that of designating the seat of one's emotions or deepest feelings, or simply to the emotions and feelings themselves. . . . Together these words refer to the entire inner being of the Christian, his emotions, affections, thoughts and moral choices.[4]

I've become convinced that God desires to transform *both* our emotions (heart) and our thought life (head), a topic to be treated in the next chapter.

Exploring Our Emotional Life

Because God is interested in our emotional life, how do we begin to grow in this area? One basic disadvantage for most of us is that we just don't know how to label our various emotions in order to easily talk about them. Like learning a foreign language, we need to acquire a new vocabulary that helps us describe our inner world. After discussing this problem with a psychologist friend of ours, Bill Roth, I developed a simple five-label checklist (which follows) that continues to help me become more aware of how I'm feeling. I reduced the range of feelings to five broad categories, using two sets of words that sound very similar for ease of memory: *glad, sad, mad,* and *dreads and dreams.* When in conversation with a spouse, roommate, or close friend, you can each talk about your day by moving through the list, first one sharing, then the other.

❑ Was I *glad* today (joyful, pleased, happy, feeling up)? Talk about it.

❑ Was I *sad* today (sorrowful, down, disappointed)? Talk about it.

❑ Was I *mad* today (frustrated, annoyed, irritated, ticked off, angry)? Talk about it.

❑ What do I *dread* (concerned, bothered, worried, anxious, fearful)? Talk about it.

❑ What are my *dreams* for the future (longings, yearnings, wishes, hopes)? Talk about it.

Many fruitful times of conversation have opened up for Beth and me by using this simple list. Make sure you share something for *each* of the categories, even if it's very brief, because it's easy to get sidetracked and just talk about the joys. The benefit of this simple practice is that it helps you move through the *whole range* of emotions.

ENGAGING IN DEEPER HEART WORK

Because our emotional reactions and outbursts give us important clues to the hidden depths of our soul, we must attend to them if we wish to make progress in growing a tender heart that is receptive to God. We are much deeper beings than the thoughts that typically come to our mind's awareness. If we think our life is basically run by our conscious thoughts, we're fooling ourselves. Our life is mostly moved along by our emotions and our character, much of which remain hidden to us.

To deal with the good, bad, and ugly experiences of life, each of us has learned—as children, teens, and adults—certain ways of coping to navigate our movement forward in life. Sadly, most of these coping strategies are sinful. Now each of us has our own set of dark and hidden compulsions, our drivennesses, our addictions, that compel us to *act* and to *react* to those around us, often ignoring the real needs and dignity of others. The main problem is that these habitual patterns *overregulate* our lives and actually enslave us, limiting God's work and grace in us.

Suddenly, a particular situation calls forth our compulsiveness, and we automatically move into *overdrive* or *overreaction*. Without real awareness, we replay a learned response to this situation so similar to ones in our past. We find ourselves compelled to act in a certain way and assume it's all good and normal, perhaps even "Christian." But actually we're deceived. As Gerald May frankly states in his insightful book *Addiction and Grace*, "To be alive is to be addicted, and to be alive and addicted is to stand in need of [God's] grace."[5] Rather than blame others for the difficulties we face, we should first consider what part of the problem lies within our own borders, as our Lord directs.

> "Why do you look at the speck of sawdust in your brother's eye and pay no attention to the plank in your own eye? How can you say to your brother, 'Let me take the speck out of your eye,' when all the time there is a plank in your own eye? You hypocrite, first take the plank out of your own eye, and then you will see clearly to remove the speck from your brother's eye." (Matthew 7:3-5)

I didn't realize I had an angry side until I read Dallas Willard's *The Divine Conspiracy*[6] and was convicted by God about my contempt for those "turkeys" and "jerks" on the freeway who couldn't wait their turn or endangered others by squeezing in front to get ahead. For the first time, these words of Jesus hit me hard: "But I tell you that anyone who is angry with his brother will be subject to judgment. Again, anyone who says to his brother, 'Raca,' is answerable to the Sanhedrin. But anyone who says, 'You fool!' will be in danger of the fire of hell" (Matthew 5:22). I asked God to help me develop a forgiving heart that would be gracious and not condemn or pour curses on my fellow arrogant and clueless drivers.

God and I got to a place where I would become aware of my outburst *just after* the event prompting it, then in the *midst* of the outburst, then just *as* I was about to give the driver a piece of my mind. Again this was a process of months of effort and of intentionally inviting God to tenderize my heart toward these drivers, sensing His conviction in my heart and bowing to His righteous ways. Finally, "graduation day" arrived about twelve months later when someone cut in front of me and I had no outburst at all. I actually remained in a state of peace throughout the event! Of course, I've had my lapses, but God's power and peace continue to uphold me on the road.

God's promise in Philippians 4:6-7 is sure: Admit and release to God our worries, our concerns, our problems, and over time, with our intentional participation through spiritual disciplines, God will transform our heart so we can be freed to experience more and more of His soothing peace.

NOTICING THE MOVEMENT OF OUR HEART

When we're in a boat on the water on a windy day, it's easy to feel the rocking or rolling movement as the waves lift up and bring down the boat. For some of us, this rolling action sets off physical sensors, and motion sickness takes over. But how adept are we at noticing the various movements and turbulence within our heart?

One classic framework identifies three basic emotional tendencies: (1) *approaching* another person to participate and engage with him or her, (2) *avoidance* or withdrawing, evading, or escaping from the other person, and (3) *moving against* another to stand our ground or defeat the other. Of course, each of these movements can be a very appropriate response within a given situation. Yet in other situations, these tendencies may launch a response energized by one of our sinful compulsions or coping strategies. These strategies are intended to protect our ego at all costs, completely overlooking the choice of reliance on God's power and grace.

How can we tell whether it's a sinful movement or a healthy one? These are complex phenomena and require mature discernment. A good start is to notice if there is that *added* energy that suddenly compels us into action. From down deep, something moves within us, taking over. It's an energy that seems somewhat out of line or beyond what would be appropriate in the situation — the punishment doesn't seem to fit the crime. Of course, in an emergency, this sudden energy can be very fitting. But at other times, it indicates a reaction beyond what the situation calls for. It's an *over*reaction.

EXTRA HELP FROM THE DARK SIDE

Our compulsions and coping strategies are not the only factors that keep us from getting good at life. As believers, we must also acknowledge the active participation of the Devil and his demons. Scripture tells us our patterns of sinful anger can become an open gate for regular demonic harassment. Paul tells us, "'In your anger do not sin': Do not let the sun go down while you are still angry, and do not give the devil a *foothold*" (Ephesians 4:26-27, emphasis added). Clint Arnold explains:

> The most natural way to interpret the use of *topos* (foothold) in Ephesians 4:27 is the idea of inhabitable space. Paul is thus calling these believers to vigilance and moral purity so that they do not relinquish a base of operation to demonic spirits. . . . When [Paul] cautions them about surrendering space to the devil, he is warning them against allowing the devil (or a demonic spirit) to exert a domineering influence in an area of their lives. For a Christian to nurture anger, for example, may grant a demonic spirit inhabitable space.[7]

When Jesus first announced to His disciples the prediction of His coming suffering and death, Peter gave Him a piece of his mind: "Peter took him aside and began to rebuke him. 'Never, Lord!' he said. 'This shall never happen to you!'" (Matthew 16:22). But Peter's sinful, negative reaction to Jesus was not energized only by his compulsions. It was also stirred up by Satan himself: "Jesus turned and said to Peter, 'Get behind me, Satan! You are a stumbling block to me; you do not have in mind the things of God, but the things of men'" (verse 23).

When we keep in perspective the continuing cosmic spiritual battle, we can recognize that our sinful actions, energized by our compulsions or coping strategies, can be stirred up even more by demonic spirits. These intensify our sinful actions and bring about further destruction and evil. We must become more aware of possible demonic involvement from our own actions, as James warns us, "But if you harbor bitter envy and selfish ambition in your hearts, do not boast about it or deny the truth. Such 'wisdom' does not come down from heaven but is earthly, unspiritual, *of the devil.* For where you have envy and selfish ambition, there you find disorder and every *evil* practice" (3:14-16, emphasis added). As a part of the process in which God tenderizes our heart to manifest more and more of the fruit of the Spirit, we'll need to battle Satan's various footholds in our life by attending to our feelings and our reactions.

Charles Kraft, who ministers in inner healing and deliverance, uses the analogy of rats feeding on available garbage to depict demonic harassment of believers. Although the Holy Spirit indwells believers forever (see John 14:16), as long as we have "garbage" in our life (for example, wounded or damaged emotions, or sinful patterns), we then give these evil spirits the entry point or "foothold" (Ephesians 4:27) to aggravate us and intensify our sinful actions and reactions. The solution is to deal with our damaged emotions and our sin in order to close off any entry points. According to Kraft, "The biggest problem is not the demons, it is the garbage."[8] Of course, we are responsible for our own sin, whether or not there is any demonic harassment. But Paul also stated that we need not be unaware of how the Enemy works and that we can resist the Devil at each temptation to sin: "Put on the full armor of God so that you can take your stand against the devil's schemes" (Ephesians 6:11). Also, "If you forgive anyone, I also forgive him. And what I have forgiven—if there was anything to forgive—I have forgiven in the sight of Christ for your sake, in order that Satan might not outwit us. *For we are not unaware of his schemes*" (2 Corinthians 2:10-11, emphasis added). And, "Submit yourselves, then, to God. Resist the devil, and he will flee from you" (James 4:7).

׀ PROPOSED MODEL OF CONFLICT RESOLUTION

After Jesus' wonderful mountaintop experience of His transfiguration, Peter, James, John, and Jesus return to find an upset father
surrounded by a crowd in debate and the other disciples who, although experienced at the ministry of exorcism, were not able to
cast a demon out of a boy. The father approached Jesus to lodge his
complaint: "I begged your disciples to drive it out, but they could
not" (Luke 9:40; see also Matthew 17:16; Mark 9:18).

Instantly, Jesus let out a very personal and emotional response,
"O unbelieving and perverse generation, . . . how long shall I stay
with you and put up with you?" (Luke 9:41). The comment conveys
frustration regarding the lack of faith of the father, of the crowd, and
even of His disciples. Jesus then dealt with the situation: "Bring your
son here" (verse 41). As the boy was being brought to Jesus, the evil
spirit threw him into a convulsion. When Jesus rebuked the demon,
the boy was instantly healed and given back to his father. Later, while
alone with His disciples, Jesus responded to the disciples' question
regarding why they could not cast out the demon: "Because you
have so little faith" (Matthew 17:20).

From this passage, consider the following general points, which
may offer some guidance for how to respond appropriately with
God's grace when facing difficulties and crises that arise with family
members, friends, fellow church members, colleagues at work, and
neighbors:

In a conflict situation, leave room for healthy emotional venting.
"Venting" suggests the letting off of internal emotional steam or
frustration. R. T. France notes that rhetorical questions, as Jesus

made in this particular situation (for example, "How long shall I stay with you and put up with you?"), "need be no more than idiomatic expressions of frustration."[9] Because Jesus never sinned (see Hebrews 4:15), His expression of frustration gives us permission also to vent our own frustrations. But we must also notice *how* He did so. He identified the object of His frustration in their lack of faith ("What an unbelieving and perverse generation!" as one commentator translates it)[10]—more of an aside to Himself—and used an "I" statement to own His feelings: "How long shall I . . . put up with you?" It's not a blaming statement beginning with *you*, although some Bible versions unfortunately interpret the emotional Greek interjection "O" as "You" here (see Matthew 17:17; Mark 9:19; Luke 9:41; see other uses, Matthew 15:28; Luke 24:25). And it's not the time for solutions yet. Now is the time for appropriate emotional expression of the pain of the one venting.

By way of application, then, to my outburst at Beth mentioned at the beginning of the chapter, if I had been honest to describe my feelings rather than play the blame game and spew all over Beth, my response to her could have been, "Oh no!" And then I would have paused as I began a new habit of describing my feelings and what my frustration was really about: "I feel so frustrated that I've got to change my schedule again this week. I'm never going to get that project done." Beth, secure in herself and without a need to defend her ego, would actively listen to my frustration, come alongside, and enter into my pain and empathize with me: "Yeah, I see how very frustrating that could be. That makes me sad too." Scripture encourages us to "mourn with those who mourn" (Romans 12:15). Of course, it will take many attempts at this kind of give-and-take to grow into a more healthy way of describing our feelings and for us to really listen to the other's venting without rising up to defend ourselves.

Together work on dealing with the immediate situation. Jesus asked for the boy, and the disciples brought him. Jesus interviewed the father about the problem and diagnosed it. He healed him and gave the boy back to his father. So, after we leave some time for emotions to be vented and affirmed, we then look at the pressing need together as partners, rather than as adversaries. Of course, honest venting and empathic listening sets the best tone to move to this second step. If we start looking at the past to fix blame, we've moved back into the mode of sinful compulsions and defense mechanisms, and we're also wasting valuable time and energy that could be used to work on the immediate problem. If there is an immediate issue, it must be addressed right away. That is the primary concern, not the history of how we got here. "So what do *we* do *now?*" We face the conflict as a team. It's *our* problem, not *your* problem. We postpone any discussions of what brought the conflict on. In our situation, because only an hour remained before Beth was going to use the car, the only solution was for me to adjust my schedule.

Later, privately and at leisure, discuss the episode and brainstorm ways to decrease a recurring problem. After the healing was completed, the disciples went privately to Jesus and asked Him why they couldn't cast out the demon. Jesus explained that it was their lack of faith. He then used the occasion to teach about faith (see Matthew 17:20-21).

Once the impending crisis is addressed in some fashion, we can agree on the best time for reflecting on the event, when emotions are calmer and the pressing need of the problem won't oppress the tone of the conversation. We can then be honest about what went wrong. Each of us can admit the part we played. If need be, we can apologize and ask for forgiveness and receive it. For those of us who tend to try to fix problems, we can then offer systematic solutions that might help prevent this kind of problem from recurring.

GODWARD OPENNESS

How then is growing deeper in our relationship with God tied with being more aware of our emotions? Honesty before God is highly valued by Him, as indicated in David's psalm of confession: "Surely you desire truth in the *inner parts*; you teach me wisdom in the *inmost place*" (Psalm 51:6, emphasis added). Gerald Wilson explains that "the instruction to assume an attitude of intimate vulnerability with God uses two unusual terms to get the idea across."[11] The first term, "inner parts," is rarely used and occurs in only one other place, Job 38:36 (NASB and NIV translate it there as *mind*). The other term, translated "inmost place," appears more often, though typically in a different context, that of "'plugging up' available water sources (wells, springs, channels) to prevent their use by another party"[12] (see Genesis 26:15,18; 2 Kings 3:19,25; 2 Chronicles 32:3-4,30). Another use occurs in Ezekiel 28:3 and Daniel 8:26, that of hiding away. Wilson draws the connection to Psalm 51:6: "God seeks open access to those parts of our lives that we have chosen to keep deeply hidden within our inner world."[13]

Now that we know God wishes us to open our deep emotions to Him, we can't go on living the same clueless way. To ignore God's invitation to open ourselves to His searching gaze would indicate a willful resistance to His loving embrace in the deep parts of our lives. Rather, as David closes Psalm 139, let us invite God in: "Search me, O God, and know my heart; test me and know my anxious thoughts. See if there is any offensive way in me, and lead me in the way everlasting" (verses 23-24).

Only recently has Psalms become personal to me and begun to help me explore this new terrain. Although it is the dynamic hymnbook of Israel, Psalms for me was mostly distant historical theology. I could make sense of the words, but I hadn't yet developed the sensitivity to enter into the wide range of emotions displayed there. "Why are you downcast, O my soul? Why so disturbed within me? Put your hope in God" (Psalm 42:5,11; 43:5).

Since becoming more aware of my own troubled soul, I am sharing more of my anxious thoughts with God and, as God promises in Philippians 4:7, I am experiencing more of His peace. Moreover, the Spirit is slowly transforming my emotional life to manifest more and more of the fruit of the Spirit, which mostly involve significant *emotional* features: love, joy, peace, patience, kindness, goodness, faithfulness, gentleness, and self-control (see Galatians 5:22-23). So, as we grow in our emotional capacities, not only can we be more honest with God, but we are also being slowly transformed by the Spirit to experience these essential Christlike affections in the depths of our soul.

As James reminds us, "God opposes the proud but gives grace to the humble" (4:6). If we remain imprisoned in our pride, God will oppose us. But if we humble ourselves before God, His grace will empower us to grow a more humble heart—a heart ready to listen to how God may be speaking to us through a variety of means.[14]

This transformation will not take place overnight. But when we give persistent effort to specific spiritual practices, God will slowly release us from our compulsions and liberate us to be whole beings, both in heart and mind. In the next chapter we take up the topic of renewing our minds.

QUESTIONS FOR PERSONAL REFLECTION
OR GROUP DISCUSSION

1. The author encourages us to develop a vocabulary for a wide array of emotions using the checklist on page 69. Think about that list of five emotions: glad, sad, mad, and dreads and dreams. Ask the Lord to bring to mind events today or this past week (or month) that prompted emotions in *each* category. If it's hard to come up with something for a certain category, consider asking someone who knows you well to help you think more about that particular category as it relates to your life. If you are married or live with a roommate, try using the list to open a deeper conversation about your life.

   a. Any surprises for you?

   b. Did you experience reactions from the person you shared with that enable you to know yourself better?

   c. Is there something that came to mind in going over this list that you would like to talk about with another person to gain more insight into yourself?

2. Anger, fear, pride. Every Christian wrestles deeply with one or more of these. Which one do you think you tend to wrestle with the most at this point in your life (and in which Satan is able to tempt you the most to sin)? Pour out your heart to God in a journal, letter, poem, or psalm, sharing with Him this tendency

and your desire that He continue to tenderize your heart. Ask Him for guidance to become increasingly released from this compulsive tendency. If it helps you to process with another, consider sharing an aspect of your journaling with a friend.

3. Look at the episode involving Jesus' frustration with His disciples (Matthew 17:14-21; Mark 9:14-29; Luke 9:37-43) along with the proposed three-step model for conflict resolution (see pages 76–79). How do you tend to resolve conflicts with others? What goes well? What doesn't go so well? What do you wish to take away from this chapter for your own practice of conflict resolution?

CHAPTER FOUR

FORMING A THOUGHTFUL MIND
STAYED ON GOD

WE CHRISTIANS SUFFER FROM TWO DISASTROUS PROBLEMS OF THE mind: First, we don't stay focused on God for very long. Second, we don't think as deeply as we should. In short, we have a long way to go in loving God with all our minds (see Matthew 22:37). But there's no point in feeling guilty about these failures. What we need are new insights into how we can grow in these two areas of the Christian mind.

First, our task is to cultivate *an ability to stay focused* on important matters throughout the day, especially on God himself. Recently, a scientific study was done on people with an extreme obsessive-compulsive disorder that manifests itself by frequent hand washing to the point of losing skin on the hands. Brain scans were taken of the people, revealing that all had an unusual neurological pattern in a specific region of the brain. Their brains had developed ruts in them, grooves associated with the disorder. Each patient was asked to meditate on positive thoughts and experiences throughout the day and to stay focused repeatedly on them. After two months, scans were taken again. To the scientists' amazement, the ruts were gone and the scans were normal. And great progress was made with the hand-washing behavior; in some cases it was totally eliminated!

Changing thought patterns, learning to repeatedly meditate on new and positive things, not only forms a new outlook on life, but also reconfigures the brain such that the old ruts that tend to drag a person down are removed altogether. For Christians, the lesson is that we can and must learn to habitually place our minds on God if we are going to see lasting change in our moods, attitudes, and behavior.

Second, a Christian mind is one that is learning to think well about all of life *from the perspective of a Christian worldview.* A person with a mature Christian mind sees what others miss and can provide deep and penetrating insights where they are lacking. This person also knows what he believes and why he believes it. This kind of confidence proves invaluable in many situations, especially when it comes to sharing the faith.

I (J. P.) am regularly saddened about how unusual it is for Christians to be taught how to think carefully about what and why they believe as they do. Judging by the Scriptures, church history, and common sense, it is clear that something has gone wrong—desperately wrong—with our modern understanding of the value of reason and intellectual development for individual discipleship and corporate church life.

The road to spiritual formation includes the development of both aspects of the Christian mind: learning to keep our mind stayed on God and learning to think well as a Christian. In this chapter, we will learn more about why these are important and how to develop both aspects.

DEVELOPING A MIND
THAT IS STAYED ON GOD

Not long ago, I had a family member in real need. On hearing this, I prayed for two continuous hours on my knees. If I had attempted this ten years earlier, about five minutes would have been all I could have mustered. How can we learn to pray intensely for long periods of time? How is it possible to pray continuously through the day?

We will tackle these difficult questions in this section. But before we begin, remember one thing: As we saw in chapter 2, the regular practice of a golf swing at a driving range or of a spiritual discipline is different from swinging in the game or engaging the practice in the crises of real life. As a real-life practice, the main purpose of prayer in the New Testament is to ask God for things we need and to receive answers. Additional purposes are confessing sin to God, worshiping, and giving thanks to Him. However, as a spiritual discipline, the purpose of prayer is quite different. What is that purpose? It is a *biblical invitation to flourishing*. Take a look at the following passages:

> I have set the LORD continually before me. . . . I will not be
> shaken. Therefore my heart is glad.
> (Psalm 16:8-9, NASB)

> Thou wilt keep him in perfect peace, whose mind is stayed
> on thee: because he trusteth in thee.
> (Isaiah 26:3, KJV)

Now He was telling them a parable to show that at all times
they ought to pray and not to lose heart.
(Luke 18:1, NASB)

Rejoice always; pray without ceasing; in everything give
thanks.
(1 Thessalonians 5:16-18, NASB)

If David, Isaiah, Jesus, and Paul agree about something, it's a
pretty good idea to listen up! Please notice two things. First, notice
the words that describe ongoing, constant prayer as a discipline
to be sustained throughout the day. Second, notice the terms that
characterize the purpose and result: a steady life of joy, perseverance,
and peace. The main function of the spiritual discipline of prayer is
*to learn how to focus our mind and whole being continually on God all day
long, so that we will grow in a steady life of joy, perseverance, and peace.*

Let's think about this fact of spiritual life: It is difficult to sin
and pray at the same time. Our little souls cannot do these at once.
In fact, the first thing we have to do in order to sin is to block God
out of our minds. If we are holding Him before our attention, it's
very difficult to do something wrong. Similarly, if we learn to be
stayed on God all day long, it will become much more possible
to have a life of joy, perseverance, and peace. The opponents of
these—depression, quitting on life, and turmoil—become ours
primarily as we experience God's distance. In light of this, growth
in constant prayer would seem to be a good thing. But is it really
possible? How can I pray all day when I have work to do, people to
talk to, things to read, and so forth? We may feel lucky to grab time

for a brief prayer now and then during our busy day. How in the world can anyone expect us to pray all the time? But remember, it was not just anyone who came up with this idea. It was David, Isaiah, Jesus, and Paul. So it must be possible to do this. But how?

How Continuous Prayer Is Possible

The answer comes when we are clear about the nature of our conscious minds. To see this, it will be helpful to employ a widely accepted analogy used to illustrate the nature of consciousness, namely, a rheostat (or dimmer switch). A rheostat is either on or off, but once it is on, it is capable of varying degrees of intensity. Similarly, a person is either conscious or unconscious, but consciousness itself has varying degrees of intensity. By way of application, our field of consciousness has a center and a periphery. If an object is in the center of our consciousness, it is the object of an act of focused awareness. But the same is not true for objects on the periphery of consciousness. If, while deep in conversation, two people have a physical object, say a picture, moved past them on the edge of their peripheral vision, they will not report having seen the object, yet they can describe it later under hypnosis. They had a peripheral awareness of the picture while their focused attention was on their conversation.

What does this have to do with ongoing prayer? Simply this: It is impossible to keep God in the center of our attention throughout the day. But it *is* possible to develop the skill of keeping God on the boundaries of our conscious attention by engaging in certain activities of prayer as a spiritual discipline. Besides yielding a life of joy, perseverance, and peace, these activities have two wonderful effects: First, they allow us to be at least mildly aware of God all day long. Second, when we take a break for intense, focused prayer, we do not have to start cold turkey. We do not bring God to the center of our attention from a state of being totally unfocused on Him. No, we bring God to center stage from already being faintly aware of Him. Therefore, it becomes much easier to intensify our focus on God and to do real work in prayer.

THREE TIPS FOR DEVELOPING ONGOING PRAYER

Here are three activities that have proven helpful to us in our engagement with prayer as a spiritual discipline, helping us develop the habit of ongoing prayer. If they do not prove helpful to you, consider developing a different strategy.

First, we recommend that you begin by saying the Jesus Prayer about three hundred times a day. Now, before you roll your eyes in disbelief, hang in there with me. Derived from Luke 18:38, the Jesus Prayer has had a powerful impact on people at various times in church history.[1] And while it comes in different forms, the wording we prefer is "Lord Jesus Christ, have mercy on me!" If you take up this challenge, I think you'll see some remarkable results.

Say the Jesus Prayer quietly out loud, because exercising your body in spiritual disciplines is crucial to forming a habit. Saying a prayer at night inside your mind does not have the impact on your life that kneeling and praying out loud has. God hears both prayers, but by regularly engaging the body, the latter will have more of a formative impact on you. You may be thinking that repeating a prayer over and over again violates Jesus' warning, "And when you are praying, do not use meaningless repetition [do not keep on babbling, NIV] as the Gentiles do, for they suppose they will be heard for their many words" (Matthew 6:7, NASB). On the contrary, the use of repetitive prayer as a spiritual training exercise does not fall under this prohibition. As New Testament scholar Don Carson said, Jesus is not

> forbidding all long prayers or all repetition. He himself prayed at length (Luke 6:12), repeated himself in prayer (Matt 26:44), and told a parable to show His disciples that "they should always pray and not give up" (Luke 6:12). His point is that His disciples should avoid meaningless, repetitive prayers offered under the misconception that mere length will make prayers efficacious.[2]

A person who practices meaningless repetition thinks that there are mystical powers in the words themselves and that if they simply say them repeatedly, the gods will pay attention and be forced to answer. Jesus also implies that meaningless repetition is done as a work—praying repeatedly in an attempt to earn the right to be listened to by God.

Proper repetitive prayer has nothing to do with earning anything or coercing God to listen. It is done solely to gain the ability to pray meaningfully for more and more of your time throughout the day. This may be why Jesus, right after issuing this warning, gave His followers a prayer—the Lord's Prayer—to memorize and regularly repeat. In fact, like training wheels on a bicycle, the more you strengthen the habit of ongoing prayer, the less you will need to use the Jesus Prayer.

Second, combine repetition of the Jesus Prayer with other texts you dearly love. Here is how to do it. As you get up in the morning, you may be in the habit of starting to worry about your day or just stumbling into the kitchen for your morning coffee. When you first awaken, say the Jesus Prayer twenty to thirty times. As you do, something will begin to happen to you. God will slowly begin to occupy the center of your attention. Once this happens, and while you move on to showering or fixing breakfast, start praying a passage of Scripture that you love, such as the Lord's Prayer or Psalm 23. After praying a phrase, pause and focus it on various aspects of your world like this: "Our Father who art in heaven; You occupy the position of authority in this universe, and I claim Your authority over my daughter today. She faces a very difficult decision about her boyfriend, so I express my confidence in You and Your protective reign over her life. I invite Your rule into this decision."

Continue to pray this phrase for other things of which you are concerned, then move to the next phrase and do the same ("hallowed be Thy name; may Your reputation be regarded as holy in my committee meeting this morning"). If you are like us, when you tried this in the past, your mind started to wander after just a few minutes. Once this happens, return to the Jesus Prayer and repeat it until you are again centered on God. Then return to where you left off in your passage and continue. In this way, the Jesus Prayer allows you to continually bring your attention to the text of Scripture you are phrase-by-phrase praying into your world. When you have to focus your attention on your morning activity, say by reading the paper or talking to someone on the phone, you can silently repeat the Jesus Prayer at the same time on the borders of your attention.

Remember, you can do more than one thing at the same time: drive while listening to the radio, talk to someone while doing the dishes, listen to the television news while reading the sports page. You can't do two things at once if both require occupying the very center of your attention, but as long as one of the acts is on the periphery while the other is more central to your awareness, you can indeed do more than one thing at once. Repetitive use of the Jesus Prayer while doing more focused things allows God to be on the boundaries of your mind and forms the habit of being gently in contact with Him all day long.

Third, seven to ten times a day, pray on your knees for two to three minutes. If you try to do this more often or longer each time, you most likely will not form this habit. If it's possible (in other words, if you have privacy), when you get to work or between appointments, drop to your knees. During a commercial break, try going to a place in your home at which you regularly pray, and kneel and pray for two minutes. During the two to three minutes, start with the Jesus Prayer five or ten times, then start praying a favorite passage into the various concerns of your life ("The Lord is my shepherd, I shall not want. Precious Lord, my friend Sally is in great financial need, so I pray a lack of need for her. Please miraculously provide the five hundred dollars she needs"). Then return to the show after the commercial.

HABITUAL PRAYER AND RECEIVING ANSWERS

Besides developing in you a life of joy, perseverance, and peace, these disciplinary practices will have another effect. When you leave the "practice field" and enter a "real game," that is, when a crisis arises that calls on you to engage in deep, focused, serious prayer to fight spiritual warfare or to bring God's power to bear on a very crucial matter, you will be able to stay focused in prayer for a long, long time. Your habitual prayer activities will keep you from becoming distracted as you focus for some time on an urgent need.

In a battle against Amalek, Israel prevailed as long as Moses' hands were lifted up. Once his hands dropped, Israel began to lose (see Exodus 17:10-13). This is not just an odd story. It teaches a profound truth about prayer. Moses' lifted hands were a form of prayer, a form of expressing dependency on God, and as his hands were lifted in prayer, this act became a conduit of God's power while he *remained* in that activity. Sometimes, it is important to learn to stay focused in prayer for long periods of time.

DEVELOPING AS A MATURE CHRISTIAN THINKER

William Law once noted that "unreasonable and absurd ways of life . . . are truly an offense to God."[3] God loves good thinking. Indeed, God is the epitome of intellectual excellence. Knowledge may puff up, but the solution to arrogance is not ignorance—it's humility. Clearly, the Bible itself places great emphasis on developing the mind as can be seen in important passages: Romans 12:2 and Matthew 22:35-40.

Paul's writings are the most complete set of biblical instructions about the nature of discipleship and how it's attained. Arguably, the most significant verse he ever penned about spiritual transformation is Romans 12:2. In this wise and tender admonition, Paul the devotional master puts his finger on the very essence of how we grow to become like Jesus: "Do not be conformed to this world," he tells us, "but be transformed by the renewing of your mind" (NASB). The term *renewing* translates the Greek word *anakainosis*, and its meaning is fairly straightforward: "making something new." The term *mind* translates *nous*, which means "the intellect, reason, the faculty of understanding."

We are so familiar with this verse that it often loses some of its unusual quality. But to see how truly peculiar this teaching is, think of what Paul could have said — but did not. He could have said, Be transformed by developing feelings of closeness with God, by exercising your will in obeying biblical commands, by intensifying your desire for the right things, by fellowship and worship, and so on. Obviously, these are important parts of the Christian life. Yet Paul chose to mention none of them in his most important summary of the spiritual life. Why is that? It is clear that, for him, how one thinks and what one honestly believes form the very core of character and transformation.

In Matthew 22:35-40, an expert in the Mosaic Law challenged Jesus to summarize the entire Old Testament. In answering this question, it is apparent that Jesus must have studied the Old Testament thoroughly. Remember, even though He was God, He was also human, and during much of His earthly life, He hid and subordinated to His Father His divine nature and lived as a genuine human being. He grew in knowledge, learned things, and so forth. His answer to the lawyer, now famous, included these words: "YOU SHALL LOVE THE LORD YOUR GOD WITH ALL YOUR HEART, AND WITH ALL YOUR SOUL, AND WITH ALL YOUR MIND" (verse 37, NASB). In other words,

God is worthy of being loved with every single facet of human personality, not simply with one or two aspects. Note that Jesus included an intellectual love for God.

These two texts emphasize the importance of how we think and, more specifically, what we actually believe, because beliefs are important for spiritual maturity. Beliefs are the rails on which our lives run: We almost always act according to what we really believe. It doesn't matter much what we say we believe or what we want others to think we believe. When the rubber meets the road, we act out our actual beliefs most of the time. That is why behavior is such a good indicator of a person's beliefs. If we're going to develop a spiritually vibrant set of beliefs, it is important to know the differences among three aspects of belief: content, strength, and centrality.

THE CONTENT OF A BELIEF

The content of a belief helps determine its importance for our character and behavior. *What* we believe matters — the actual content of what we believe about God, morality, politics, life after death, and so on, will shape the contours of our life. In fact, the content of our belief is so important that our eternal destiny is determined by what we believe about Jesus.

Today people are inclined to think that the sincerity and fervency of our beliefs are more important than their content. All that matters is our sincerity, we are told. Nothing could be further from the truth. Reality is indifferent to how sincerely we believe something. I can believe with all my might that my car will fly me to Hawaii, but that fervency doesn't change a thing. As far as reality is concerned, what matters is not whether I like a belief or how sincere I am in believing it, but whether the belief is true. I am responsible for what I believe and, I might add, for what I refuse to believe, because the content of what I do or do not believe makes a tremendous difference in what I become and how I act.

THE STRENGTH OF A BELIEF

If you believe something, that does not necessarily mean you are certain it's true. It means that you are at least more that 50 percent convinced it's true. If it were just fifty-fifty for you, you wouldn't have the belief in question; you would still be in a process of deciding whether or not you should adopt the belief. A belief's strength is the degree to which you are convinced the belief is true. As you gain evidence and support for a belief, its strength grows for you. It may start off as plausible and later become fairly likely, quite likely, beyond reasonable doubt, or completely certain. The more certain you are of a belief, the more it becomes a part of your very soul and the more you rely on it as a basis for action.

There is an important practical application of this point. When you assess what it is you really do and do not believe—say, on a solitude retreat—it is important to include in your assessment how strongly you accept the important beliefs in your life. Your strategy for growth is not simply to come to have the correct beliefs. Just as importantly, you should seek to strengthen the important beliefs you already have. To strengthen your beliefs, talk to others who embrace them and let their confidence strengthen you, read defenses of those beliefs, find answers to objections, and act as though you strongly embrace the beliefs, even if you don't. One way beliefs may be strengthened is to practice acting on them.

THE CENTRALITY OF A BELIEF

The centrality of a belief is the importance of the role the belief plays in your entire set of beliefs—that is, in your worldview. The more central a belief is, the more your worldview will be affected if the belief is given up. My belief that prunes are good for me is fairly strong (even though I don't like the belief!). But it isn't central for me. I could give it up and I would not have to abandon or adjust very many other beliefs I hold. But my belief in absolute morality, life after death, or the Christian faith are very central for me—more central now, in fact, than just after my conversion in 1968. If I were to lose these beliefs, my entire set of beliefs would undergo a radical reshuffling, more so now than, say, in 1969. As I grow, these beliefs come to play a more central role in the entire way I see life.

By way of application, try to have truly important beliefs at the center of your life, because your central beliefs determine your character more than less central beliefs. It will help to (1) inventory your central beliefs, (2) work at making sure your core beliefs are really important and true, and (3) develop stronger convictions about them. If you work at this, your life will become less scattered and more peaceful at the center; a calm stability will grow inside you.

HOW DO WE CHANGE BELIEFS?

In sum, the content, strength, and centrality of a person's beliefs play a powerful role in determining the person's character and behavior. But here is an apparent paradox about our beliefs. On the one hand, Scripture holds us responsible for our beliefs; it commands us to embrace certain beliefs and warns us of the consequences of accepting other beliefs. On the other hand, experience teaches us that we cannot choose or change our beliefs by direct effort. For example, if someone offered you ten thousand dollars to believe right now that a pink elephant is sitting next to you, you could not really choose to believe this in spite of having a good motive to do so.

Happily, there is a way out of this paradox: We *can* change our beliefs *indirectly*. If I want to change my beliefs about something, I can embark on a course of study in which I choose to think regularly about certain things. I can read certain pieces of evidence and argument, and I can try to find problems with evidence raised against the belief in question. More generally, by choosing to undertake a course of study, meditation, and reflection, I can put myself in a position to undergo change in the content, strength, and centrality of my beliefs. My character and behavior will then be transformed by those changes. That's why Paul says to be transformed by the *renewing of the mind*. This insight naturally leads to a discussion of the spiritual discipline of study.

THE SPIRITUAL DISCIPLINE OF STUDY

A spiritual discipline is "an activity undertaken to bring us into more effective cooperation with Christ and His Kingdom."[4] In any human endeavor, repetitive exercise and practice bring skill and excellence. Sometimes a particular activity is good because it accomplishes a specific result. Swinging a baseball bat is good if it produces a base hit. However, that same activity can also be done, not for the result alone, but for the training that it offers. A person can go to a batting cage and repeatedly swing a bat for the purpose of training, but not with the purpose of getting a base hit. And other good results can follow from such training besides the one usually or normally intended; for example, regular trips to a batting cage can get a person in good overall condition besides helping him or her get base hits.

The same thing is true of study. We often approach an activity of study for some direct purpose, such as preparing a lesson or learning about a topic. But study should also be approached as a training activity, as spiritual and intellectual exercises. Study is a discipline that strengthens the mind and enriches the soul. Sometimes I study a book for the sheer value of engaging my intellect in a stretching, strenuous activity. At other times, I read to help myself cultivate certain intellectual virtues, such as becoming nondefensive, seeking truth, knowing why I believe what I believe. Seen as a discipline, study becomes a means of building my character, ingraining habits of thought and reflection, and reinforcing the life of the mind.

We study, then, not simply to gain knowledge about the topic of study, but as a broader spiritual discipline. By way of application, it is important to read books from time to time as a form of spiritual discipline and intellectual exercise, even if the topic of a given book does not address one of our immediate, felt needs. If all we do is read simple books and those that overemphasize stories or practical application, we will never learn to think for ourselves as mature Christians, nor will we develop trained minds.

THREE TIPS FOR THOUGHTFUL READING
Learning to read thoughtfully is important for the spiritual discipline of study. Thoughtful reading is an attempt to grasp the concepts,

structure, and arguments that form the content of a text being read. The goal is to learn something new, to master a specific content, to develop intellectual categories, and to grow in the ability to think. Space forbids me to describe this sort of reading in detail, but three things are important for developing skills in this type of reading.

The mind works from *whole to parts to whole*. First, when you start to read a book or begin a new area of study, get an overview of the main issues in that book or area of thought. For example, in reading a book, you can begin by reading the jacket or the introduction in order to get a grasp of the book's primary thesis and the main issues being discussed. Next, spend a few minutes studying the table of contents. Use a pen to note on the page any observations about structure you can see (for example, that chapters 1 and 2 seem to go together and chapters 3 through 5 contain answers to the problems discussed in the first two chapters).

For college students or those who have access to a good library, if you are really going to dissect a book, obtain a few book reviews of it prior to your own reading. When I bought my textbooks for the semester in graduate school, I would go immediately to the library, ask the librarian for help in locating reviews of these textbooks (they are trained at doing this), and photocopy and read them. Today you can often find reviews on the Internet. A good book review gives you the book's thesis and overall structure, and evaluates the strengths and weaknesses of the book. Both can be helpful to have in mind before you begin to read. Your purpose in all of this is to get a tentative grasp of the whole of the book and at least some feel for how the author develops her thesis.

Second, after these initial steps, begin to read the book with pen in hand. Move from your tentative guess at the book as a whole to an examination of the book's parts. If possible, never read a serious book without pen or pencil. Your goal in reading is to discover the structure of each chapter. Of course, once you have read the book's parts, you can reexamine your initial guess at its overall thesis and structure, and revise where necessary.

When you approach a new area of study, start with a brief introduction to the subject. For example, read dictionary definitions or encyclopedia articles. Locate an introductory textbook in the area and read it first. A librarian can help you find a magazine or journal article that summarizes the main issues in the area of study. Again, your goal is to obtain an overview and an initial set of categories that can help you notice things you may otherwise miss when you set out to analyze a topic in more detail.

Third, in addition to the movement from whole to parts to whole, focus on *structure* at each step, especially when you are involved in actually reading a chapter of a book. I usually take a pen and—every two to three paragraphs—write in the left margin a summary of the main arguments in the text. I am careful to note in the margin any change in the structure. For example, I ask these kinds of questions: Is the author continuing to develop the same point of discussion treated in the preceding paragraphs? Has the text shifted to making a new point parallel to the one just made, or are we now involved in reading criticisms and rebuttals of the main thesis? What you are after is a chapter filled with marginal notes that form an outline of the flow of that chapter.

After I read a subsection in a chapter (usually marked off by an actual subheading in the text), I return to the page where it began and write a two- to three-sentence summary of the main point of the subsection. When I have finished the entire chapter, I look at all of my subsection summaries and write a summary of the entire chapter at the top of the first page of that chapter. Here's the point: You want to mark a book in such a way that if you return to the book months later, you can look at your notes and easily remember the main points of the chapters.

INTELLECTUAL READING AS WORSHIP

We can cultivate the art of intellectual reading as part of personal worship. Here are three things to keep in mind: First, do not measure the value of such reading by the immediate practical application or spiritual enlivening that comes from an hour or two devoted to analyzing a chapter or two of a book. Often it takes several chapters for an idea to be developed with sufficient care and depth to have something to apply to life and thought. Sometimes you'll need to be patient and stay with a line of thought for several weeks before things get clear to you. Intellectual reading is not a quick fix, and its value is measured in the long-term maturity that comes from practicing it.

Second, get into the habit of reading books that are somewhat beyond your ability to grasp. If you spend all of your time reading things that require little intellectual effort, you will not stretch your mind and grow appreciably in your thinking ability.

Third, when you undertake to read a book seriously, you cannot treat that book as a novel to be read for recreation. Compared to intellectual reading, recreational reading is fairly passive, it can be done quickly, and it does not require a great deal of work or engagement on the part of the reader. In intellectual reading, you simply must stay alert, use a pen, make notes regularly, and remember to look for three things: Structure! Structure! Structure! If you do not walk away from an occasion of reading with a better grasp of the flow of argument—the logic structure—in what you read, you have not practiced intellectual reading successfully.

A mature Christian mind thinks skillfully about all of life from a biblical perspective and has the developed ability to stay focused on God throughout the day. Furthermore, a growing Christian mind begins to recognize the truths and promises of Scripture. As already mentioned in the discussion of prayer, we want to grow into a deeper trust and reliance in our God, who does the impossible. In the next chapter, we'll develop that theme a bit further.

QUESTIONS FOR PERSONAL REFLECTION
OR GROUP DISCUSSION

1. As a way to try out the suggestions on thoughtful reading, think about the following (you may need to look back over the chapter to answer the questions):

    a. What two subjects were presented in this chapter?

    b. Which spiritual disciplines were recommended?

    c. Consider writing a two- to three-sentence summary of the contents of the chapter. (You may want to continue this practice for the rest of the chapters.)

2. God has made our minds with wonderful powers of concentration and awareness. Do you tend to use any of the principles mentioned in this chapter in other areas of your life (for example, preparing a presentation, remembering something)? What will you take away from the chapter to help you pray more?

3. What does the author recommend we do to change and strengthen our Christian beliefs? What key area of study and practice can you identify to work on and grow in?

CHAPTER FIVE

FORMING A TRUSTING WILL
THAT RISKS WITH GOD

GETTING GOOD AT LIFE MEANS TAKING RISKS—SOMETIMES, HUGE risks. In Jesus' parable of the talents (Matthew 25:14-30), a landowner who decides to travel far away entrusts to three servants different amounts of his wealth: To one he gives five talents, to another two, and to a third one. During the landowner's absence, the first two servants invest these funds in business ventures and double their money. But the third servant buries his talent in the ground because he is fearful of losing it and earning the wrath of the landowner, whom he distrusts. When the landowner returns, each servant explains his business dealings. The landowner praises the first two servants for risking his money and investing it wisely, but he severely scolds the third servant for his laziness.

Previously, I (Klaus) hadn't paid close attention to the amount of a talent until a Bible teacher pointed out that for an average person, two talents was basically equal to a lifetime of wages.[1] That thought made the parable personal for me. In a rapid but profound paradigm shift, I realized that Jesus expects each of us to invest the substance of our lifetime—all we are and all we have, whether two talents or many more—for the kingdom of God. What a risk! And yet, as we shall see, Jesus takes pains to teach us to trust Him with our lives and our fortunes.

Think for a moment of how many of God's people in the Bible took great risks to follow Him. For example, Abraham and Sarah left all that was familiar to them and set out not knowing where they were going—led only by God. But they rested in God's great promises (see Hebrews 11:8). Rahab took a risk to protect two spies and trust in their God, and after the battle of Jericho, God honored her faith (see Joshua 2:1-2; 6:23-25). Gideon led the Israelites into a battle against the Midianites and Amalekites as obvious underdogs, yet God promised them victory (see Judges 7:1-22). King David, at risk of losing his life and of possibly never ascending the throne, waited for God's timing to become the official king of Israel. On two occasions David had golden opportunities to take matters into his own hands by killing King Saul, but he didn't rush ahead of God's timetable (see 1 Samuel 24:1-25; 26:1-25).

In the New Testament, Mary risked her future, her reputation, even her relationship with Joseph, her fiancé, to accept the divine gift of pregnancy and bear the Christ child. And the apostle Paul constantly risked his life as he traveled to share the good news with others. He wrote,

> Three times I was beaten with rods, once I was stoned, three times I was shipwrecked, I spent a night and a day in the open sea, I have been constantly on the move. I have been in danger from rivers, in danger from bandits, in danger from my own countrymen, in danger from Gentiles; in danger in the city, in danger in the country, in danger at sea; and in

danger from false brothers. I have labored and toiled and have often gone without sleep; I have known hunger and thirst and have often gone without food; I have been cold and naked. (2 Corinthians 11:25-27)

More than anyone on earth, our Lord Jesus Christ was a risk taker. The second person of the Trinity willingly diminished His divine glory to take on the limitations of humanity and live among us as an ordinary carpenter and religious teacher. No flash. No expensive entourage. No five-star hotel reservations. No pampered life. And He did all this knowing He would be ridiculed, mocked, scourged, tortured, and put to death on a cross. But from God's point of view, *it was all worth this risk*. The future glory of His grand project of creating a home of righteousness for us all was worth the pain—even for God himself.

All these men and women stepped out in faith and accomplished what they had never done before, carried along by God's grace and power. But what is expected of us? Remember that God has given each one of us at least "two talents" to invest in this life. So the question is, How will we use our talents? What risks are we willing to take with what Jesus has entrusted to us, so that when He returns, we can present to Him much more than we began with? In the parable, the landowner promised to his risk-taking servants, "You have been faithful with a few things; I will put you in charge of many things. . . . Come and share your master's happiness" (Matthew 25:21,23).

In a more recent story, a young woman named Kelly took a risk with God by handing over her last laundry coins to a more needy friend.[2] Kelly, a young, single mother, lived with her five-month-old son, Eric, in public housing. Sundays she would push his stroller to the little white church on the corner, where, holding him close, she worshiped God and heard God speak to her now and again through the pastor's sermons. Another weekly habit was setting her dirty laundry on the back of Eric's stroller to head for the local Laundromat.

One afternoon, while Kelly sorted dirty laundry at home, her friend Lisa knocked on the door. With tears in her eyes, Lisa shared that she had no money and her kids had no clean clothes. Could she borrow some laundry money?

If Kelly were to give her own laundry change, she wouldn't be able to clean her clothes that week. The Spirit brought to her mind the Sunday sermon about Jesus' challenge, "Give, and it will be given to you. A good measure, pressed down, shaken together and running over, will be poured into your lap. For with the measure you use, it will be measured to you" (Luke 6:38). The pastor's charge had been, "Remember, Jesus gave His all; He gave His very life! When you are asked to give, give as the Lord did. Give until it hurts!" With a measure of hesitation, Kelly handed the change to Lisa and thought to herself, *It hurts, Lord!*

After Lisa left, Kelly threw her piles of dirty laundry back into the hamper and slumped into a chair, pondering her situation. In a couple of days, it would be Mother's Day. Kelly's first Mother's Day. But it would be celebrated without a husband for her and without a father for Eric.

Soon the phone rang. The pastor explained that he had just been praying, and Kelly's name had come to mind. "Do you know of anybody who could use a free washer and dryer?" he asked.

"I sure do," Kelly responded. "Me!" The pastor and his wife had bought a new washer and dryer, yet the old ones still worked fine. Kelly then shared the rest of her story—how she had been prompted to give till it hurt and how meaningful this gift was. God had multiplied her laundry money into her own washer and dryer.

The appliances arrived the day before Mother's Day. For Kelly, they are a continuing reminder of God's faithful provision.

ON LOAN FROM GOD

Ultimately, not one of our possessions is permanent. We really do not own a thing, because we can't take it with us after we die. Job said it this way: "Naked I came from my mother's womb, and naked I will depart" (1:21). Or, in the words of the apostle Paul, "We brought nothing into the world, and we can take nothing out of it" (1 Timothy 6:7). Letting that thought sink into our minds will help us look at life with new eyes. We can focus on what really matters. As in Jesus' parable of the shrewd manager, we can use the goods of this life for things that last. Jesus said, "I tell you, use worldly wealth to gain friends for yourselves, so that when it is gone, you will be welcomed into eternal dwellings" (Luke 16:9).

The talents God gives to each of us in differing proportions—our bodies and minds, for example, and the particular situations in life in which we find ourselves—are just temporal aspects of life. We can't even take our present physical bodies with us. So, because these temporal resources are simply on loan from God, we are freed to take appropriate risks.

GETTING THE BIG PICTURE

If someone recommends a movie or novel to us—but explains how the story ends—the surprise is spoiled. But the eternal story is different. God's revelation of how history ends makes all the difference in the world for those of us living now (see Revelation 21–22). In the future, God will permanently take up residence in the midst of His people (see Revelation 21:3; Jeremiah 31:33). He will be our God, and we shall be His people. Believers will experience the fullness of the glorious presence of God: "They will see his face" (Revelation 22:4; see also Numbers 6:25; Isaiah 25:9). In the future, God's kingdom will finally and fully come to earth—the very thing the church has longed for and prayed about for millennia. Matthew wrote, "Your kingdom come, your will be done on earth as it is in heaven" (6:10). It will be a new day with "a new heaven and a new earth" (Revelation 21:1), no darkness (see 22:4-5), and no more pain, mourning, or death (see 21:4). Furthermore, we will serve God and reign with Him forever and ever (see Daniel 7:18,27; Revelation 3:21).

If life consisted only of our time on this earth, what a bleak prospect that would be! Of course, there is much good here, but evil continually ruins the good God has created. The great news is that our ultimate destiny is with God, where evil is banished and good always flourishes. As Peter informed us, "But in keeping with his promise we are looking forward to a new heaven and a new earth, the home of righteousness" (2 Peter 3:13).

Because God's victory is certain, so is our future. We can actually look forward to physical death and being "at home with the Lord"

(2 Corinthians 5:8). At some point believers will individually stand before the "judgment" (read "award ceremony") seat of Christ, where each of us will receive Jesus' blessing and assessment for how we lived our years here on earth (see 2 Corinthians 5:10; compare 1 Corinthians 3:12-15; Matthew 25:14-30). At last, God will create a new heaven and earth (see Revelation 21:1) and God "will dwell among them, and they shall be His people, and God Himself shall be among them" (Revelation 21:3, NASB). And finally will come the main event in all of God's program: what has been called the Vision of God or the Beautiful Vision. We shall see God face-to-face (Revelation 22:4) and not die (Exodus 33:20).

Why ponder these future realities? G. K. Beale notes that God reveals to us these aspects of the future to encourage us in the present: "The prophetic vision of the perfected people of God in unending fellowship with him (Rev 21:1–22:5) is intended to comfort and motivate God's people to persevere through temptations."[3] Consider Paul's word of encouragement: "For I consider that the sufferings of this present time are not worthy to be compared with the glory that is to be revealed to us. . . . For in hope we have been saved . . . but if we hope for what we do not see, with perseverance we wait eagerly for it." (Romans 8:18,24-25, NASB). Maintaining a future focus is essential for living now. As C. S. Lewis commented, "Aim at heaven and you get earth thrown in. Aim at earth and you will get neither."[4]

MORE REAL THAN THE PHYSICAL REALM

Six-year-old Emily Wiechman is partially handicapped due to a stroke at seven months old. While on vacation, driving with her parents and grandparents through the little-populated regions of Wyoming, Emily suddenly started vomiting and her eyes weren't focusing. Her parents turned their van toward the hospital in Rock Springs, seventy miles away. Time was of the essence because Emily was slowly getting worse.

As they neared the town, Emily's mother, Marlene, prayed that God would direct them quickly to the hospital. Very soon, her eyes caught a blue-and-white hospital sign confirming they were going in the right direction. Three signs later, they arrived at the emergency room, where the doctor diagnosed Emily's problem as a seizure. He was able to stabilize her with anticonvulsants.

Later Marlene told the doctor that without the hospital signs they wouldn't have found the hospital so quickly. The doctor asked, "What signs?" He drove to and from the hospital each day along that road; it had no hospital signs. After leaving the hospital, they retraced their route. Even though all four adults in the van had seen signs earlier, no signs were there. Even checking with the chamber of commerce verified that no signs had been placed on that route. Marlene now acknowledges, "I believe they were put there for us by God or his angels."[5]

There is much more to life than the visible world. An invisible realm of reality exists beyond our physical senses that is more *real* than what we can see, touch, taste, hear, or smell. God and His angels exist in that immaterial realm. And we also exist and interact in that realm, because we are not just physical bodies. We also have an immaterial soul or spirit that can commune with God. Paul reminds us of these two components of our existence; the outer part is physical and the inward part is immaterial: "Therefore we do not lose heart. Though outwardly [that is, our physical body] we are wasting away, yet inwardly [that is, our immaterial spirit] we are being renewed day by day. . . . So we fix our eyes not on what is seen, but on what is unseen. For what is seen is temporary, but what is unseen is eternal" (2 Corinthians 4:16,18). James said it another way, in explaining physical death: "The body without the spirit is dead" (James 2:26).

GETTING READY FOR THE FUTURE

Have you ever considered what you will need in the afterlife? The Egyptian kings of the past gave a lot of thought to how they would live in the afterlife. Some built glorious tombs—the pyramids, for example—to gather the treasures they hoped to use in the next life. Within the tomb of King Tutankhamen (who reigned from 1333–1323 BC) were found clothes, furniture, weapons, a chariot, and a number of other objects.[6] But sadly, it was all left behind; he never got to use it.

Although we may enter eternity *empty-handed*, we do not enter *empty-hearted*. What can we take with us? Consider these permanent items from the immaterial realm of reality:

- We can take with us our *friendships*—most importantly our friendship with God, but also with our fellow humans in God's family. In heaven, we will continue to get to know God, building on the relationship we've cultivated with Him here. And we'll continue in the relationships in the body of Christ that we've grown here, just as the disciples took up where they left off when they met Jesus after His death and resurrection (see John 21). This is God's marvelous kingdom community. We will explore friendships more fully in the final chapter of this book.

- We can also take with us our *good deeds,* or at least the effects of our good deeds on others. In the parable of the talents, the landowner rewarded the servants for their faithful management of his money and said, "Well done, good and faithful servant! You have been faithful with a few things; I will put you in charge of many things. Come and share your master's happiness!" (Matthew 25:23). We can engage in kingdom work by doing good to overcome evil and to invite "outsiders" to become members of God's eternal family.

- Finally, we can take with us our *character,* the kind of person we're becoming. We'll continue learning and building on what we've gained here in knowledge and wisdom, in skill and talent, in attitudes and desires—all purified from any taint of evil.[7] We are becoming the kind of citizens God desires to populate His eternal kingdom, citizens for whom Paul wrote, "Train yourself to be godly. For . . . godliness has value for all things, holding promise for both the present life and the life to come" (1 Timothy 4:7-8).

Another way to highlight what we can take with us is offered in the following illustration, in which five enduring kingdom themes are presented within layers of concentric circles. The central theme is our relationship with God. Jesus emphasized this foundational part of our lives in summarizing Deuteronomy 6:5 from the Hebrew Bible: "'Love the Lord your God with all your heart and with all your soul and with all your mind.' This is the first and greatest commandment" (Matthew 22:37-38). The remaining four themes are based on Jesus' second command: "Love your neighbor as yourself" (verse 39; quoting Leviticus 19:18).

FIVE ENDURING KINGDOM THEMES

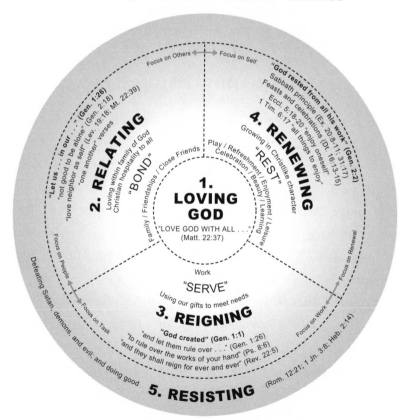

The next circle directs our attention to the important themes of our relationships within God's family ("love one another," John 13:34-35), our service to meet the needs of others through work and ministry ("serve one another in love," Galatians 5:13), and attending to the formation of our own character ("train yourself to be godly," 1 Timothy 4:7).

Finally, the outer circle reminds us that we must do good to defeat evil ("Do not be overcome by evil, but overcome evil with good," Romans 12:21). We can use these various circles for "target practice" for eternal investing. The aim is to be engaged in some way in each of these important kingdom values, accomplishing God's work and laying up treasure in heaven along the way.

WORTH THE RISK?

But is it really worth the risk? Why not just wait till Jesus comes and let Him make all things right? The Bible offers several reasons to be actively engaged in kingdom work and values now. First, as chapter 1 pointed out, only in pursuing God's way now can we enter into a deep and lasting kind of happiness in this world. The abundant living Jesus promised in John 10:10 only comes when we follow Jesus' good wisdom on what life is all about (see, for example, Matthew 7:24-27).

Second, God is preparing us now to reign with Him in the future "for ever and ever" (Revelation 22:5). He's using our experiences here as a school of leadership to train us in how to reign with Him. But first He wants to help us learn how to reign and how to wisely use our resources. As we engage in kingdom values and His good work, we develop the leadership competencies we will need for eternity. Remember, the landowner promised future leadership responsibilities to the faithful servants: "I will put you in charge of many things" (Matthew 25:23).

God has also supplied various resources for His kingdom work. The greatest gift is the Holy Spirit, the divine Helper (see John 14:16; Luke 11:13), who actually indwells every believer and sanctifies us. Yet the Holy Spirit also empowers us with ministry skills or "spiritual gifts" to serve others (see Romans 12:3-8; 1 Corinthians 12; 1 Peter 4:10-11). Teaching, helping, giving, and showing mercy are among these (see the lists in Romans 12 and 1 Corinthians 12). We can regularly engage in letting God's love flow through us by the use of our gifts in our local church, in our neighborhood, and even overseas in some needy situation. We can live beyond our physical human resources, but only if we increase our reliance on the Spirit.

Jesus expects us to take risks and be busily engaged in kingdom work now, just as He taught in the parable of the talents. He challenges us to keep a future focus—an eternal perspective—as we live here below: "Do not store up for yourselves treasures on earth, where moth and rust destroy, and where thieves break in and steal. But store up for yourselves treasures in heaven. . . . For where your treasure is, there your heart will be also" (Matthew 6:19-21). How we live our life and the good we do will be reviewed at what is called the Bema Seat of Jesus, something like an award ceremony. Paul wrote, "For we must all appear before the judgment seat of Christ, that each one may receive what is due him for the things done while in the body, whether good or bad" (2 Corinthians 5:10).

Teaching on rewards for believers is evident throughout the New Testament. We have already mentioned Jesus' statement about storing up treasures in heaven (Matthew 6:20). Earlier in Matthew 6, Jesus mentioned that our efforts in participating in Christian practices can be honored either by others or by God himself: "Be careful not to do 'acts of righteousness' before men, to be seen by them. If you do, you will have no reward from your Father in heaven" (verse 1). From whom would you rather receive your reward? Consider the following smattering of verses on rewards:

> "And if anyone gives even a cup of cold water to one of these little ones because he is my disciple, I tell you the truth, he will certainly not lose his reward."
> (Matthew 10:42)

> The man who plants and the man who waters have one purpose, and each will be rewarded according to his own labor.
> (1 Corinthians 3:8)

> Whatever you do, work at it with all your heart, as working for the Lord, not for men, since you know that you will receive an inheritance from the Lord as a reward.
> (Colossians 3:23-24)

> "Behold, I am coming soon! My reward is with me, and I will give to everyone according to what he has done."
> (Revelation 22:12)

It seems that God is willing to make it worth our while to expend the effort to seek His kingdom and do what is right, despite the opposing forces railing against us. Because of the extra difficulty entailed by the evil we must battle in this world, perhaps we might view rewards as a kind of "hazard pay"—an extra incentive for engaging in such dangerous work. As martyred missionary Jim Elliot so eloquently stated, "He is no fool who gives up what he cannot keep, to gain what he cannot lose."[8]

FAIR PLAY?

We may be concerned that not all believers truly have an equal opportunity if we have varying resources allotted to us by God during this lifetime. Maybe we would have had a better life and done more kingdom work if our family had been wealthier. Or maybe we would have been better in sports if we had been a little taller or stronger. Or maybe we would have gotten a better education or better job opportunities if we had lived in a different part of the country or the world. Can't we all think of someone who seems to have gotten more than what seems to be his or her fair share? And what about those who have received what appears to be less? When we look around us, didn't the third servant in Jesus' parable have a point: that the landowner might be untrustworthy? Is God really fair in how He distributes His resources? How can God hold us accountable for the way we invest our lives on this planet, if the resources to succeed are dished out differently?

A key lesson from the parable of the talents is to be faithful with *what God has given*. The three servants were each entrusted by the landowner with differing amounts. When the landowner returned to learn of each one's stewardship, he praised the faithful stewards *equally,* although each brought the master different amounts of returns (see Matthew 25:21,23). God sovereignly assigns our resources, and they will differ according to His wise plan. The question we each must answer is not "Why did God give that brother or sister more than me in this area?" but rather "What am I going to do with what I've got?"

Another lesson from the parable is that we must trust God for His sovereign goodness and wisdom in our use of His resources. In a sense, the landowner in the parable represents God. The fault the landowner found in the third servant was his fear—his inability to risk. The servant assumed that that landowner was fickle (verse 24), and he didn't inquire more deeply into the landowner's character. If he had, he would have learned that the landowner was a rewarder of earnest faith (see Hebrew 11:6). It was a lack of risking—not a risky investment—that earned the landowner's wrath.

As followers of Christ, we have a tendency to focus on avoiding sins of commission, that is, steering clear of activities we *should not* be doing. Yet the parable of the talents reminds us also to become equally concerned about sins of omission; that is, we can also do wrong by not doing something we *could* be doing. As James taught, "Anyone, then, who knows the good he ought to do and doesn't do it, sins" (4:17). Of course, we must avoid letting anxiety from an overscrupulous conscience (or from our compulsions) overwhelm us, wrongly assuming we have godlike omnipotence and must have our fingers in every kind of activity throughout the world. Most of the time, we're just clueless—no twinge of conscience or anxiety, not even aware of the good we could be doing if we would take more wise risks with God's resources.

EXAMPLES OF OTHER RISK TAKERS

We grow in our faith by engaging in kingdom work beyond what seems possible, obeying kingdom values, and relying on God's empowering grace. As Dallas Willard notes, "The cautious faith that *never* saws off the limb on which it is sitting never learns that unattached limbs may find strange, unaccountable ways of not falling."[9] For example, one kingdom value revolves around generosity and sharing our financial resources. Jesus Christ affirmed that "it is more blessed to give than to receive" (Acts 20:35) and said, "Freely you received, freely give" (Matthew 10:8). When Moses challenged the Israelites to make contributions for the new tabernacle, the spirit of giving stirred deeply in their hearts. The people were so generous that Moses had to order them to stop giving (see Exodus 36:6-7)!

As of 1997, despite an annual income rising above $30,000 only with overtime as a postal worker, Thomas Cannon had given away more than $96,000.[10] He awarded thousand-dollar grants to honor those who do good deeds, such as a group of teenagers who rescued a drowning horse and a Junior Women's Club that had adopted a school near Cannon's home.

More amazing is Matel Dawson Jr., who by age seventy-six had used his frugal savings and investments to give away over $800,000.[11] Based solely on his salary as a rigger and forklift driver at a Ford Motor Company plant, Dawson donated three apartments he owned (worth a total of $30,000) to a charity for the homeless and gave $240,300 to the United Negro College Fund, $200,000 to Wayne State University, $100,000 to Louisiana State University, and $107,000 to his church. And he isn't finished yet. "My goal is to help LSU again" with a $100,000 scholarship.

FAITH-STRETCHING PRAYER AND PROJECTS

How has God been stirring your heart to respond to Jesus' faith-stretching challenge posed in the parable of the talents? Here's a thought experiment that can be done right now in the quiet of your heart. Have an imaginary garage sale in your mind for *everything* you own. Wave good-bye to some of the biggest items as they are purchased and carried off. Now imagine living without them. Could you really do it? What hold does each object have on you?

Which of our material things can we not part with? We may ridicule the ancient Israelites for having foreign idols in their households (see 2 Chronicles 15:8), but do we have any modern-day idols among our possessions? The apostle John wrote, "Dear children, keep yourselves from idols" (1 John 5:21).

In a different arena, for those of us who are parents, have we truly given our children to God? Or is there still a hook of possessiveness? We can entrust their lives to God, for they are given to our care for only a brief period.

Where will you step out of your comfort zone to be a blessing to others? Perhaps the first step might be to get more acquainted with others who have grown in their faith by trusting God for great things. Read the biographies of Christian leaders (for example, Billy Graham, Bill Bright, or Henrietta Mears) and watch videos portraying such faith in action (such as *Luther, The Cross and the Switchblade,* and *Chariots of Fire*).

Perhaps the following exercise will help you assess how your "eternal investment portfolio" is doing. For each of the five enduring kingdom themes, there is a list of a couple of general questions to give you an opportunity to rate your involvement. You can't improve every area at once, but why not pause now to take pen and pad out and make a list of three to five faith-stretching projects for the next year? Of course, invite God to help you identify what to do and how to pray specifically. Develop a range of projects, some with high risk for you and some low risk. I urge you to make this part of God's School of Faith for your life.

How's My
ETERNAL INVESTMENT PORTFOLIO (EIP)
Doing?

How well am I investing now in my future eternal life as God empowers my life? Rate from "1" (little being done) to "7" (doing well).

1. Living in the very presence of God and sensing His love and affection — **Loving God**

    1 2 3 4 5 6 7   How well am I regularly connecting with God (more than before) in all that I do?

    1 2 3 4 5 6 7   How well am I mulling over in my mind verses from God's Word?

2. Living in God's loving community of brothers and sisters in Christ — **Relating**

    1 2 3 4 5 6 7   How well am I deepening my close Christian friendships (i.e., "one anothers")?

    1 2 3 4 5 6 7   How well am I reaching out to others in hospitality and humility?

3. Serving God and others with my talents/gifts to be a leader in God's kingdom—**Reigning**

    1 2 3 4 5 6 7   How well am I using my talents/gifts to meet needs and build others up?

    1 2 3 4 5 6 7   How well am I growing at becoming a servant-leader like Jesus?

4. Developing a soul and character rested and perfected in God—**Renewing**

    1 2 3 4 5 6 7   How well am I engaging in "activities" that really renew my soul like Jesus did?

    1 2 3 4 5 6 7   How well am I working on forming my character with God's grace?

    1 2 3 4 5 6 7   my thoughts?
    1 2 3 4 5 6 7   my feelings?
    1 2 3 4 5 6 7   my behavior?

    1 2 3 4 5 6 7   How aware am I of working at humbling myself and watching prideful thoughts?

    1 2 3 4 5 6 7   How aware am I of my sinful "compulsions" that harm myself and others?

5. Defeating Satan and evil and doing good—**Resisting**

    1 2 3 4 5 6 7   How well am I minimizing Satan's many influences in my life?

    1 2 3 4 5 6 7   How well am I helping those in need of my advocacy for good?

The parable of the talents reminds us that we are only managers of God's resources. Because we come with nothing into this world and leave with nothing materially, all the material goods we have come only from His hand. We have the opportunity to enjoy them and share them with others, and soon they'll be gone. Now we are but "aliens and strangers in the world," as Peter depicted our journey in this world (1 Peter 2:11). It's a real paradox, because the more heavenly minded we become, the more useful we are on earth for God's purposes. When we understand that, we can no longer bury our talent and do nothing. We're freed by God's grace to risk, stretch our faith, and invest our "two talents" in the true ideals of loving God and loving our neighbor as ourselves.

Of course, we'll experience times and seasons of our lives when God will not provide and will not show up as we expect Him to. On these occasions God will seem very hidden. Why? We'll explore that issue in the next chapter.

QUESTIONS FOR PERSONAL REFLECTION
OR GROUP DISCUSSION

1. What do you really own? If, as Paul said, "we brought nothing into the world, and we can take nothing out of it" (1 Timothy 6:7), why do we tend to get so caught up in our possessions (clothes, car, house, bank accounts, other "assets") that they start possessing us?

2. Jesus' parable of the talents poses the challenge that Christians must take wise risks in this life with what God loans us. Why do we so often play it safe? Do you think it's wise to risk with God? Do you risk "to a degree" or do you risk everything?

3. Look back at the illustration "Five Enduring Kingdom Themes" on page 117 and the exercise "How's My Eternal Investment Portfolio (EIP) Doing?" on pages 125–126. Review the five themes: loving God, relating, reigning, renewing, resisting. Do you think that our Christian life should involve some engagement in each of these themes? Which themes seem to be ones you tend to emphasize more? Might there be harm (or something lacking) for believers who do not engage in all five themes in some way? Are there any other themes you might add?

4. How are you planning for eternity? Read through the exercise again. Does one theme or particular item stand out as something you would like to emphasize for further growth? What might

you specifically do over the next month to make an eternal investment there? Or perhaps you'd like to come up with two or three faith-stretching prayer projects in which to persevere in prayer over the next twelve months.

CHAPTER SIX

EMBRACING THE
HIDDENNESS OF GOD

HAVE YOU EVER WONDERED WHY GOD HIDES HIMSELF? DOESN'T HE want everyone to know Him in this world? Maybe God should hire a better public relations firm.

We can't deny our experience: God seems to hide Himself. Of course, there are those special moments when the heavens open and something unusual takes place. Sometimes God lets His saints peek into the heavens to see great and glorious realities. For the prophet Ezekiel, "the heavens were opened and I saw visions of God" (1:1). Stephen, the first Christian martyr, said this as he was being stoned to death, "I see heaven open and the Son of Man standing at the right hand of God" (Acts 7:56). And the apostle Paul "was caught up to paradise. He heard inexpressible things, things that man is not permitted to tell" (2 Corinthians 12:4).

Every believer eventually will see God face-to-face. All things will be open to view at the end of history, when the eternal new age begins (see Revelation 22:4). But here and now we live in a time of God's partial hiddenness, where we are in some sense "absent from the Lord" (2 Corinthians 5:6, NASB). It's a time when even our own lives are "hidden with Christ"; that is, we are now hidden even to ourselves; we aren't fully aware of who we are in Christ (Colossians 3:3-4). But, when Christ returns, all that we are will be fully revealed in glory, just in the way a beautiful Monarch butterfly emerges from its unremarkable cocoon. For now we're in our hidden form, like a caterpillar, waiting for that spectacular day of transformation.

HIDE AND SEEK?

But why is God hidden now? Perhaps this simple analogy might open the way to understand the seeming madness in God's method. I (Klaus) have fond memories of playing hide-and-seek as a child. A family picture album records one of my better hiding places: I had squeezed myself onto a hallway closet shelf, arms and legs arranged like a pretzel and with a wry smile on my face. Because I enjoyed the game, I carried on the tradition with our children.

My kids taught me that the best part of the game was *being found*. Sometimes they weren't hidden all that well. As many parents do, I'd walk around intentionally avoiding them, wondering out loud where they could possibly be. But then, at the very moment I "uncovered" them, it was all smiles—the joy of being pursued and the joy of being found. That may be the simplest and best insight into God's hiddenness in this world. Believers should continue to respond to God's initiatives of love by pursuing and "finding" Him each day.

An event in the life of Jesus directs us toward this insight. After His resurrection, Jesus suddenly joined two disciples who were walking toward the town of Emmaus (see Luke 24:13-32). Throughout the whole journey, His identity was hidden from them. The disciples were puzzled and sorrowful over the death of Jesus, but the stranger who joined them explained what Scripture taught about the Messiah—that He had to suffer and then enter His glory. While He talked, their hearts were warmed, even though they didn't know it was Jesus. As the sun set and the exciting conversation on the road came to a close, the trio arrived at the village.

Luke's record of this encounter offers one of the most puzzling statements in the Gospels: "As they approached the village to which they were going, *Jesus acted as if he were going farther*" (24:28, emphasis added). If we were in a similar situation, wouldn't we have asked the two for a place to sleep overnight—perhaps on a bed or couch? But Jesus didn't do that. Despite being their Lord, He didn't presume upon His companions but waited for *their* invitation of hospitality. New Testament scholar I. Howard Marshall explains: "The stranger made as if to proceed further. . . . He is merely giving them the opportunity to invite him in, and will not force his presence on them."[1]

The account continues: "But they urged him strongly, 'Stay with us, for it is nearly evening; the day is almost over.' So he went in to stay with them" (verse 29). Jesus waited for their invitation to spend the evening with them. He wanted to be wanted, just as any person does. He wanted to be pursued.

This unusual verse was used by God to draw a Russian soldier to Jesus Christ during the time of the Communist invasion and occupation of Romania, which began in 1944. Pastor Richard Wurmbrand and his wife, Sabina, who eventually were jailed because of their ministry, welcomed the influx of Russian soldiers into their country as an opportunity to share the love of Christ. Piotr was one Russian whom God saved. The young man then became involved in the underground church movement. One day Pastor Wurmbrand asked Piotr about how God had brought him to receive Christ. Piotr responded,

> Shortly after I met you, you read a passage from Luke 24, telling the story of Jesus meeting the two disciples who went toward Emmaus. When they drew near the village, Jesus acted as though He would go farther (verse 28). I wondered why Jesus would say this. Surely He wanted to stay with His disciples. Why then would He say He wanted to go farther? Then I understood Jesus was being polite. He wished to be very sure that He was desired. And when He saw that He was welcomed, He gladly stayed with them. I know that the communists are not so polite. They entered our hearts and minds through violence. They forced us to listen to their ideology. If we do not agree with them, they beat us. But Jesus respects our freedom. He knocks gently on the door of our heart. He has won me with His politeness.[2]

ROOM TO SEEK

Perhaps it is a measure of God's grace and kindness to hide from us until Christ comes again. For, in His unusual way, God leaves plenty of room for each of us to freely pursue Him on our own initiative—not just because we have to, but because we really want to.

God didn't have to arrange life in this particular way, so that we actually had a choice in the matter. He could have designed humanity so that both our hardware and our software were programmed to love God mechanically. Just as in a toy factory, all of us could have been programmed to proclaim our prerecorded praises. Pull the string and we'd chirp in unison, "I love You, God. I thank You, God." That way we would automatically love God, whether we wanted to or not. But that's not friendship; that's playing with toys. That kind of an arrangement wouldn't satisfy any of us, nor would it satisfy God. Any genuine friendship requires that both parties willingly seek each other in love. It just can't be coerced. God desires that kind of love relationship with all of His children, one in which we freely seek and pursue Him on our own, desiring to grow in our relationship with Him.

Have you considered how important physical space is to us, especially in a group of strangers? We like to keep our distance in conversations with others. Of course, other cultures may permit a much closer proximity—with people almost in each other's faces. But that's not typical in the Western world. When we get on a crowded elevator, our space becomes pretty cramped. We keep our distance by all facing the same way, looking up at the floor indicator. In a similar way, we tend to maintain a level of relational distance in our relationships with others. We don't like those who demand our time or are overly possessive. In a sense, God gives His followers the "space" we desire to relate with Him as we wish.

But how does a majestic, infinite, and ever-present God develop a growing love relationship with people who are frail and finite human beings? How can God develop a mutually loving friendship with believers without forcing us into it, without using divine strong-arm tactics? Acting just like a gentleman, God doesn't force His full presence on us but partially hides Himself to encourage a genuine and continuing response of friendship. God gives us the relational space we need to develop a real friendship. Think about it: The God of the universe is willing to cloak His greatness so He won't overwhelm us or coerce our friendship. That's another paradox: God must *hide* in order to *reveal* Himself to us.

But we shouldn't misinterpret God's intentions, thinking this relational distance means He doesn't care about us. Quite the opposite. God has been dreaming about cultivating a deep, personal relationship with each one of us for eternity. And He has been willing to pay the ultimate price to make this relationship possible—through the death of His Son Jesus on the cross, for "in him and through faith in him we may approach God with freedom and confidence" (Ephesians 3:12). The majestic, all-powerful God woos us to Himself through His humility, weakness, and complete self-giving. But He continues to hide Himself to give us the room we need to freely respond to His love and grow into a deeper relationship with Him. So, the goal of God's hiding is to experience the joy of being pursued, of having us draw near to Him as James 4:8 urges us: "Come near to God and he will come near to you."

THE COST OF TRUE RELATIONSHIP

Good relationships—such as the one we seek with God—don't just happen. They take effort and persistence. How much effort would you invest if you thought a certain person was worth pursuing? Consider an actual situation involving Bill Gates.

With the explosion of the personal computer market, Gates became a multimillionaire almost overnight. When he began

Microsoft, he was a Harvard dropout and computer genius in his early twenties. With this sudden wealth, he was thrust into the national limelight as a very eligible bachelor. Finally, at the age of thirty-eight, on New Year's Day 1994, he lost this status by tying the knot with Melinda French, a thirty-year-old business manager at Microsoft.

Now back to our question: How much effort would you invest if you thought a certain person was worth pursuing? Place yourself in a situation similar to that of Bill Gates before he was engaged to Melinda French. Imagine you are a very eligible, multimillionaire bachelor (or bachelorette), and you're now interested in finding and settling down with that special person who is to become your life companion. How would you go about doing that? Would you place an ad in the *USA Today* personals section?

> WORTH MILLIONS, young single seeks companion to share life in marriage.

Would that work? Not exactly, because you've got a major problem that no simple ad will solve. Because you are worth millions, how will you know that the person you are dating really loves you, not just your money? How can you be sure that it is genuine love that motivates this person to marry you, rather than the ulterior motive of getting rich quickly?

But Gates isn't the only one with such risks. There is Someone who is so wealthy, so powerful, and so smart that He can have anything His heart desires, anything He wants in the world. And, just like Gates, this Person also wants to find genuine lifelong companionship. This wealthy, powerful, and wise personal being is God, the Creator and sovereign King of the universe.

What did God do to win us to Him? He "emptied" Himself of His great wealth, His glory, and His divine privileges and came to earth as a baby, dependent on human beings. In fact, He "made himself nothing, taking the very nature of a servant, being made in human likeness" (Philippians 2:7). Further, He submitted Himself to death—the most horrible death imaginable in the first-century Roman world—at the hands of those whose love He longed for. Rather than impressing us with His wealth, "He chose the lowly things of this world and the despised things—and the things that are not—to nullify the things that are" (1 Corinthians 1:28).

When we choose to love God, we also choose "the way of the cross." In that way, our mutual love—God's and ours—is not based on what we can *get* but on what we can *give*, for only self-giving is true love.

IF GOD REALLY SHOWED UP

Even though God is infinitely good, "he isn't safe," as the famous story from C. S. Lewis's Narnia tales reminds us.[3] So, should we fear God's appearance in our lives? Even the apostle John felt fear before the resurrected Jesus. While on the Isle of Patmos, he met the Lord of glory, and although he was Jesus' best friend before the Resurrection, he reported, "When I saw him, I fell at his feet as though dead" (Revelation 1:17). And when angelic messengers suddenly appear, they must always assure their human audience with words familiar from Christmas plays, "Fear not" (see, for example,

Luke 1:12-13; 1:26-30; 2:9-10). And so God tones down a measure of His glory so that we can come near. Brennan Manning captures well the purpose of God's hiddenness. Listen in on the conversation between Willie Juan, a young boy, and the Medicine Man, who portrays the resurrected Jesus.

> "But why didn't you come to the cave with trumpets and angels and a great big show?"
>
> "I didn't want to frighten you, my friend. If I came displaying all the glory of El Shaddai, you would find it utterly unbearable and, more importantly, you'd be afraid to come close to me. Isn't it difficult to be a friend to someone who has all the answers, who's always totally unafraid, invulnerable, needing nothing and nobody, always in control of every situation? With a person like that you don't feel comfortable or needed."[4]

God's way of working is not always obvious or stunning. Much of the time, He is so subtle. As Jack Deere warns us, "God's humility is both a blessing and a very great problem. A blessing, because his humility leads him to fellowship with people as low as we are. A problem, because his humility leads him to come to us in ways that make it easy for us to reject him."[5]

BLOCKS TO SEEING GOD

But there are other hindrances to our pursuit of God. An important one that we encounter daily in an often spirit-numbing way is the concrete reality of this world. Have you ever considered how all of nature just keeps on running like the Energizer Bunny—day in and day out, predictable, regular, constant—as if it were a perpetual-motion machine requiring no outside source of power to keep it going? From a purely physical point of view, it looks as though no God is needed.

The secular worldview that we call naturalism has codified this particular fact into an assumption: All that exists is only physical. It's the only thing many scientists study. All events of life, all objects on this earth, including humans, they claim, can be fully explained by the natural laws of science. Sadly, we Christians are children of our culture and have been educated and mentored to imbibe this view deeply into our souls. Prior to the Enlightenment and the domination of the evolutionary view of origins, most people assumed God was the center of the universe and that He was involved in their daily lives. Since then, the normal view is that physical matter is the center of the universe, and that's all there is.

The mass media also play a powerful role in shaping our worldview. Serious thinking about God is not displayed as a typical American experience. However, the rare occurrences of religious comments prompt wide viewer response. Tim Russert of NBC's *Meet the Press* closed an Easter Sunday segment with these lines: "It's a beautiful day in Washington. The sun is shining; the cherry blossoms are out. Christ is risen; Yahweh is coming. And the Orioles' opening day is tomorrow." He later reflected, "I got more letters from people saying they had never heard that language on TV before."[6]

The overpowering naturalistic view of life cannot but have a disastrous impact on believers' confidence in God's presence and activity. We become convinced that God is irrelevant to daily existence.

Of course, there is a powerful but hidden conspiracy behind this movement to distract Christians from keeping God at the center of our thoughts: God's hiddenness also leaves room for the influence of Satan. How easy it is to succumb to Satan's lies, which draw us away from God and move us toward fear, oppression, and despair. Our ultimate enemy isn't the media or any particular group of human persons, but Satan himself and his myriad demons. In Ephesians we find this statement: "For our struggle is not against flesh and blood, but against the rulers, against the authorities, against the powers of this dark world and against the spiritual forces of evil in the heavenly realms" (6:12).

If we do not guard our hearts (see Proverbs 4:23), a constant tendency of our minds will be to unwittingly imbibe the lies of Satan. Dallas Willard notes, "Ideas and images are, accordingly, the primary focus of Satan's efforts to defeat God's purposes with and for humankind. When we are subject to his chosen ideas and images, he can take a nap or a holiday."[7] It is important for us to attend to the kind of self-talk we entertain in our minds. Remember Jesus' parable about the rich fool? The fool was acquiring such a great harvest for himself that he planned to build new barns, yet without any thought about his stewardship before God. Notice his self-talk.

> "What shall I do? I have no place to store my crops." Then
> he said, "This is what I'll do. I will tear down my barns and
> build bigger ones, and there I will store all my grain and
> my goods. And I'll say to myself, 'You have plenty of good

things laid up for many years. Take life easy; eat, drink and
be merry.'"(Luke 12:17-19)

There was no thought about God in all of his planning. However,
God said to him, "You fool! This very night your life will be demanded
of you. Then who will get what you have prepared for yourself?"
(verse 20).

What kind of self-talk goes on in our minds? What lies of Satan
do we entertain? Is one the thought that we are worthless and
unworthy of God's grace, and so we tend to avoid God? Or is it
that our situation is so hopeless we despair of life altogether? Do
we secretly feel we are losers because we keep on making the same
mistakes or returning to the same sin patterns? Are we overwhelmed
by fear of what might happen or of what others might do to us?
Are we consumed by self-loathing because we don't seem to fit in
anywhere the way others seem to do so easily? Do we believe we
are not making a distinct contribution to society? Or do we feel all
alone in the world, feeling that no one loves us or cares about us?

By giving in to these lies, we encourage the presence of Satan
and his influence, and we experience the absence of God and a lack
of His power in our lives. To displace Satan's lies and naturalistic
worldview that imprison us, we need to be reminded of God's
truth, the truth that will liberate us from the shackles of rejection,
of unworthiness, of despair. In the next chapter, we'll deal more
specifically with facing the trials of anxiety and depression. However,
here we want to look at a simple little method I've learned to break
the hold of this day-to-day feeling of God's absence from our lives.

THE PAUSE THAT REFRESHES

Although I begin my day with prayer and Bible reading, I still catch myself at various times in the day very much *alone* in my thoughts. Perhaps it's a result of schooling. I remember hearing these words: "Do your work alone; don't look at anyone else's paper." Through elementary school, junior high, high school, and college, we were taught mostly to do our work alone. If you're like me, you've become used to plowing through projects, checking off items on to-do lists, getting from here to there, spending much of the day without inviting God into the present moment.

We can change this pattern through the advice of Brother Lawrence (1611–1691), author of the classic devotional *The Practice of the Presence of God.* Although his duty was to wash the pots and pans in his monastery's kitchen, he was able to develop a vibrant and intimate walk with God. His secret? Taking regular breaks throughout the day to offer a quick word to God. In the spirit of 1 Thessalonians 5:17 — "pray continually" — he kept his mind stayed on God. In Brother Lawrence's words,

> Since you are not unmindful of the fact that God is present before you as you carry out your duties, and you know that He is at the depth and center of your soul, why not stop from time to time, whatever you are doing — even if you are praying aloud — to adore Him inwardly, to praise Him, to beseech Him, to offer your heart to Him, and to thank Him?[8]

In chapter 4 of this book, J. P. spoke of the wonderful benefits of the Jesus Prayer as a way to keep our mind focused on God throughout the day. Both J. P. and I encourage the practice of 1 Thessalonians 5:17 in whatever method works for you. I believe each person has freedom to customize this biblical practice in a different way.

One method I've discovered has yielded amazing results for me. I'm sure you're familiar with the pause button on a video machine or DVD player. If you're watching a movie and the phone rings or someone comes to the door, you press the pause button. To resume watching the movie, you press the button again. One day I thought, *What about pressing the "pause button of life" now and then?* The idea is to just stop what you're doing and take thirty seconds—like a commercial break—to have a word with God, the Sponsor of Life.

Why not try it out now? Simply focus your attention on God and talk with Him for about thirty seconds. Or just be still and invite God's peace to wash over you. Close your eyes now and . . . pause. . . .

How was it? I've been sharing this simple practice with others, and after trying it for a few weeks, many have discovered they've entered into a new level of conversation with God. My friend Christine began pausing to talk with God, and here's what she said she learned: "I realized I needed to spend more time with God, and the pause button gave me the time needed. I even found I had more time than I expected to develop a relationship with the Lord. This insight has made me more diligent and effective in spending time with the Lord."

The pause button practice has also helped William to connect with God in a closer way:

> This thirty-second pause in my life has given me a closer
> and more personal relationship with God. The pause button
> has created a direct line of communication between God
> and me, communication without interruption and prayer
> that is without flowery words. The pause button has actually
> enhanced my prayer life in a more focused direction that
> yields positive results.

Another friend, Jason, has combined the pause button with saying the Jesus Prayer.

Jesus himself paused a lot. Despite the press of the daily activities of ministry to others, He would often pause to visit with God: "Yet the news about him spread all the more, so that crowds of people came to hear him and to be healed of their sicknesses. But Jesus often withdrew to lonely places and prayed" (Luke 5:15-16). Scripture even records what Jesus said in a brief pause with God: "Father, glorify your name!" On this special occasion, a voice from heaven thundered, "I have glorified it, and will glorify it again" (John 12:28). Even though we may not hear a heavenly voice, we can be certain from the promises of Scripture that God hears us. Jesus said, "Look at the birds of the air; they do not sow or reap or store away in barns, and yet your heavenly Father feeds them. Are you not much more valuable than they?" (Matthew 6:26). We can be confident that God bends His ear to listen to our prayers, to our praises, to our confession, to our requests, to our joys, to our sighs, to our outbursts, to our tears.

I think God wants us to *initiate* these pause breaks, these times of conversation with Him. Consider the point in another context.

One expression of love is a kiss on the cheek. Which means more to you: a kiss you have to ask for (as grandparents might do with a grandchild) or a kiss offered freely and spontaneously—without asking—just because a person wants to? Of course, we love because God "first loved us" (1 John 4:19). He made it possible for us to have a relationship with Him by providing for our salvation and drawing us to Himself. But any ongoing relationship always requires each party to seek out the other. So God desires that we continue to seek Him now that we are children in His family. Pressing the pause button is one way to do this. At the beginning of the day, I pause and invite God to walk with me. And throughout the day, as I think of it, I pause and connect with God regarding what's going on in my life.

How do you like to remember something important? I'm a visual person. I need to see something to "get it." So, I usually write it in my daily scheduler. But I also find I write on little sticky notes. I want to use this idea of the sticky-note reminder to help you press the pause button of life. Do you happen to have some small sticky notes handy? Consider trying the following system during the rest of this week, or adapt it to whatever works best for you.

On a small sticky, draw a circle and write the word *pause* in the middle, something like this:

Then, make a few more stickies and place them at key visual spots in your path during the day—on the bathroom mirror, refrigerator, computer screen, car dashboard. Some of us need a bit of physical involvement for this practice, so actually pressing the "button" helps out. Jason did this and responded,

> This practice was hard to remember to do at first, but I took the suggestion to physically press something to get my mind to focus on God's nearness. Once I began to purposefully do this, I started to see how important that step was to helping me engage. It took about three weeks before I started to see any effects from this spiritual discipline. By the third week, it began to take on special importance. Then, it became a sanctuary in the midst of my busy life and a place that I wanted to enter more often. The greatest benefit of this practice has been to remind me that God is always there to interact with me.

As I mentioned above, Jason also included repeating the Jesus Prayer during his pause times (see J. P.'s discussion in chapter 4).

My friend Jennifer found her days filled with more peace after the pause. "The simplest way to lower my stress is to press the 'pause' button of life in any stressful moment," she said. "By pressing this button, I can go to the Lord and ask Him for His mercy to lighten my burden. Then I feel less stressful and more powerful to solve my problems."

This is a simple method, and of course it has its limitations. But if you combine it with a daily quiet time of prayer and Bible reading, I think you'll find that rather than trivializing your relationship with God, it will enrich your love of Him and immediately bring to your mind His presence in the midst of a busy day. The stakes are high — Satan and secularism are alive and well wherever we go — so we need to connect regularly with God.

TAKE A GOD-WALK

As we've been saying, God's hiddenness and invisibility pose a problem for us because we tend to be *over*whelmed with the physical side of reality and *under*whelmed with the very real but invisible God who is always near. As the psalmist proclaimed, "If I rise on the wings of the dawn, if I settle on the far side of the sea, even there your hand will guide me, your right hand will hold me fast" (139:9-10). We looked at the pause button. But how can we further personalize God's omnipresence, not just on Sunday but during each day of the week while at work, at school, or at home? Let us suggest two key practices for connecting with God.

First, be on the lookout for physical evidences of God each day. Romans 1:20 teaches that "since the creation of the world God's invisible qualities — his eternal power and divine nature — have been clearly seen, being understood from what has been made." We can marvel at God's artistic flair in glowing sunrises and blazing sunsets. We can enjoy luxurious green grass and air alive with singing birds. God is the engineer-artist who makes things functional and beautiful at the same time. What we identify through our five senses — sight, hearing, smell, taste, touch — are gifts from God for our pleasure in this life.

Scientists tell us that the secondary qualities of beauty (for example, color, aroma, sound) are not necessary for the world to operate. All we need are the primary qualities to make the world go 'round (for example, mass, energy, physical shape). God could easily have made a colorless, odorless, soundless, tasteless world that would have functioned just fine. But He didn't. He added these secondary qualities for our enjoyment, so that our human spirit would not be crushed by the world's drabness. I distinctly remember a time this truth deeply touched me. I was walking by a rose bush when that wonderful scent overwhelmed me and tears welled up as a heartfelt response to God's pleasurable gift of such a sweet smell.

Second, be on the lookout for those "coincidences" — seemingly random acts of goodness that come our way from God. Speaker and author Cynthia Heald shares about a time when she felt God was not really interested in her daily life. But God quietly replied to her discouragement in a moment of prayer, "You don't realize how committed I am to you." So Cynthia responded, "Lord, make me aware of Your work in my life." Later she attended a Christian conference with her husband. The keynote speaker was a Christian leader she highly respected. Cynthia wanted to meet him and talk a bit with him, but after the sessions, so many people surrounded him that it never worked out. Then, one morning they were driving to the conference grounds for breakfast, and they stopped to ask a couple if they wanted a ride. It turned out to be the speaker and his wife. They had a great time of conversation at breakfast. Soon after, God touched Cynthia's heart with these words, "That meeting was from Me."[9]

We must ask God to help us become more aware of the many times He touches our lives. They often come by surprise, and some seem rather ordinary. For instance, at a public library sale I "happened" on a few outstanding, out-of-print books—one of which I now use as a textbook for a class. Discovering that particular book at just the right time was a gift from God to meet that pressing need.

Of course, there are more fantastic stories. An engagement ring lost off the west coast of Sweden was found and returned two years later. The ring had been consumed by a mussel that turned up in a shellfish caught by a fisherman.[10] In God's kingdom, there are no coincidences: The good that comes our way is from God (see James 1:17).

I urge you to keep a journal. Record "coincidences" and times of God's creative presence. Sometimes capturing an event in writing can cement it in our mind and make God's presence much more vibrant. You may also want to journal about the kind of self-talk you've been experiencing, especially when it's discouraging and destructive. By getting it down on paper, you are more open to seeing the lie for what it really is: Satan's attempt to defeat you. As we continue to write, we invite God to let His truth in, so it can wash over us and cleanse us. Jesus said, "If you continue in My word, then you are truly disciples of Mine; and you will know the truth, and the truth will make you free" (John 8:31-32, NASB).

Being aware of God's presence and intervention in our lives is always important, but it is especially critical when we fall into the deep valley of depression and hopelessness. We will explore this in greater depth in the next chapter.

QUESTIONS FOR PERSONAL REFLECTION
AND GROUP DISCUSSION

1. If you were God's adviser, what advice might you give Him on ways He might be more present in this world? For example, every day could begin and end with an angelic host in the sky, singing aloud praises to God (as they did on that first Christmas night). After brainstorming several ideas, ponder the reasons God may have decided *not* to do these kinds of public things on a regular basis.

2. At His second coming, Jesus will appear with such pomp and circumstance that "every knee will bow" (Philippians 2:10, NASB). Yet, this side of heaven, it seems God has partially toned down His public glory so that His presence is not so prominent. If indeed this is the case, how does that make you feel? The author says that by remaining hidden now, God provides the relational space so we can freely seek Him. Do you agree?

3. When we leave our minds in neutral or are distracted from God, Satan has the opportunity to present various lies. Are there certain lies that tend to move around in your mind now and then? What is the specific truth that addresses each lie?

4. Several spiritual disciplines were suggested in this chapter to help you become more aware of God's ever-presence: pressing

the pause button throughout your day, taking a God-walk to notice God's creation, and journaling on "coincidences." Is there one you will try out this coming week?

CHAPTER SEVEN

DEFEATING TWO HARDSHIPS OF LIFE: ANXIETY AND DEPRESSION

WHILE I (J. P.) HAVE ALWAYS LIVED WITH A CERTAIN AMOUNT OF anxiety, I have spent most of my life without the more severe type of anxiety attack or serious depression. A year ago, however, all that changed. I found myself overwhelmed by a set of major stressors that sent me spiraling into an emotional tailspin.

The combination of stressors—two related to our extended family, another concerning an unexpected financial burden, then the discovery of the body of a friend who died from alcoholism—all ganged up to overwhelm my emotional resources. Further, I was diagnosed with a rare skin disease that placed me at high risk for colon and genitourinary cancer. Not only did I have more than twenty lesions removed from my face, I also underwent a lengthy surgery to graft skin onto my nose.

To top it off, I was worn out from work, having driven myself hard in teaching and related speaking ministries for over fifteen years. I longed for the summer months to take a break from the busy school year. But my weekly structure of work blinded me to the fact that I wasn't dealing with my mounting inner turmoil and anxiety from all these stressors. When the structure was removed at the end of the school year, everything caught up with me. I crashed and burned. My anxiety grew too great for me to handle, and I descended into a very dark time of deep depression.

I began to wake up at two or three o'clock in the morning with a racing heart and an anxious sweat. I couldn't get back to sleep. During the day, I experienced the tightness of anxiety throughout my chest and stomach. I tried to control my fears subconsciously by obsessing on one or two of them. But then I began to fear irrational things, such as getting fired or losing my home. I was afraid of life. And, because this was new territory for me, I didn't know what to do. I got to the point where it took great effort for me to do simple things like answer the phone or pay the bills. I never became suicidal, but I reached a point where I didn't care if I lived much longer. Everything I'd done in life—such as my work in teaching, publishing articles, and speaking—all seemed useless to me.

LOOKING FOR HELP

My anxiety and depression lasted seven months, but that dark time would have lasted much longer had I not taken some steps to pull out of my tailspin. With the help of a wise counselor and my own reading, I began to think through the factors that were overwhelming my ability to cope.

First, and perhaps most obviously, there the issue of overwork. Coupled with my stressful circumstances, I simply ran out of emotional and mental resources. Second, during this time some deep childhood fears began to surface. I realized I was raised in a context of fear, anxiety, and depression. My father had battled cancer for six years and died when I was in second grade. When I knew him, he was always depressed. My mother, already an anxious person, became increasingly nervous and fearful during those years.

Third, I found I had developed second-order anxiety. That is, I started getting anxious about getting anxious. I would wake up feeling decent to average, but then—at the first feeling of slight anxiety—I would begin to worry that I wasn't going to have a good day. That anxiety about my worsening anxiety would sink me deeper into fear and depression. I began to believe that things would never change, that they would never become normal again. My family became affected by my daily ups and downs, and close friends began to worry about me. Ironically, I began to worry about their worry.

These three big factors came to light as I read on the subject of depression and as I sought out people who could help. During my research, I was surprised to learn that anxiety and depression are widespread in America. Rates are rising significantly for signs of major depression (for example, appetite or sleep disturbance; feelings of hopelessness or worthlessness; significant fatigue or loss of energy; agitation, restlessness, irritability; difficulty concentrating or making decisions; frequent thoughts of death or suicide). Especially among female baby boomers—those born between 1946 and 1964—the chances of getting seriously depressed are up 65 percent compared to previous generations.[1]

But it may be getting worse for later generations. In their book *Healing Anxiety and Depression,* released in 2003, Drs. Daniel Amen and Lisa Routh claim, "Anxiety and depression are major public health problems reaching epidemic levels in the United States."[2]

These problems affect thirty-eight million Americans each year, and suicide is the eighth leading cause of death in the United States. Many of us have faced or will face serious depression or anxiety during our lifetime.

The conditions of modern life are incredibly stressful. Today "normal" life in America is brimming with stressors. However, it is not stress itself that causes anxiety and depression. Rather it is our failure to have effective coping mechanisms in place to allow us to process stress in a healthy manner. Further, it's important to know that God can use our stress to bring about good in our lives. As we proceed in this chapter, we'll be looking at three important arenas for intervention: our physical bodies, psychological issues, and spiritual aspects.

While I'm not a psychologist or psychiatrist, I want to share what has helped me deal with my depression and anxiety, along with some practical advice on stress management. Even if you are not experiencing these symptoms now, I can't emphasize enough how important it is to be aware of these factors so that you can help yourself or support a friend or a family member who is going through the dark valley of depression.

BODY AND SOUL AS A WHOLE

Too often we Christians think of depression and anxiety as a distinctly spiritual problem resulting from a defective character and weak will. We think the solution is greater trust and obedience toward God. There are, indeed, profound spiritual aspects to depression and anxiety, but we must address the problem holistically—from the physical, psychological, and spiritual perspectives.

In the Old Testament, God addressed Elijah's malaise holistically. After Elijah's famous battle with the prophets of Baal on Mount Carmel, Queen Jezebel threatened to kill him. Fearing for his life, he ran alone into the desert to hide and "prayed that he might die. 'I have had enough, LORD. . . . Take my life; I am no better than my ancestors'" (1 Kings 19:4). Elijah fell asleep and was awakened by an angel of the Lord to eat some baked food and drink from a jar of water. He slept again and was awakened later by the angel to eat again. Once he had returned to physical fitness, Elijah journeyed to Mount Horeb, where God addressed his psychological and spiritual needs (see 19:8-21).

We too must approach our situation in a holistic way. Consider the story of Dale and Jean Lasch, whose firstborn son, Peter, was diagnosed with autism at the age of three and a half. Jean prayed for Peter and asked for God's intervention as she began searching for information about the disease. She happened on a report that claimed some forms of autism are caused by sources not routinely considered, such as allergies or yeast growing inside the stomach. Jean began experimenting with Peter's diet, eliminating certain kinds of food. Astonishingly, by the third day Peter spoke for the first time. "All of a sudden he was there," Jean said. "He started to become engaged and give us eye contact. I saw a normal kid for a second."[3] Though his mental development was that of an eleven-month-old, within two years he was ready to enter school with his age-mates.

THE PHYSICAL ASPECTS OF ANXIETY AND DEPRESSION

Studies indicate that anxiety and depression usually go together, and in fact there are at least seven different kinds of anxiety/depression combinations. In some cases, anxiety and depression are purely results of brain dysfunction. But more generally, there is a physical element as well that requires care and treatment.[4] After all, we are not disembodied minds but embodied souls. What can we do?

We can begin by paying careful attention to our diet and exercise. Regarding diet, remember that certain foods can act as drugs and can be mood elevators or depressors. For example, a high-carbohydrate diet can cause blood sugar and insulin-level fluctuations to aggravate moods, energy levels, and the ability to concentrate. (For a helpful treatment of natural dietary supplements and ordinary dietary interventions relevant to treating anxiety and depression, we recommend Amen and Routh's book *Healing Anxiety and Depression*.)

Regarding exercise, two things are important: adequate aerobic exercise and strength training. A dear Christian sister and friend of ours suffered an eighteen-month debilitating bout of anxiety and depression ten years ago. Among a small handful of factors that brought her out of it and has sustained her for ten years has been a dedication to intense exercise for thirty to forty-five minutes five days a week. We recommend this too (but be sure to consult with your physician first). Brisk walking, jogging, or bicycling increases oxygen to the brain and enhances the release of endorphins in the brain. Endorphins help to elevate our mood and sense of well-being.

Weight training or some form of exercise or labor that tears down, restores, and strengthens muscles helps as well. This exercise helps to regulate the level of serotonin in the brain, something critical for eliminating anxiety and depression. Isn't it interesting that the Hebrew Scriptures elevate the importance of manual labor? God made us so that hard physical labor—whether at work or by way of exercise—restores the brain and increases our sense of well-being.

MEDICINE AND YOUR BODY

Along with maintaining healthy routines in diet and exercise, we also believe it is very important, especially for anxiety and depression, to seek proper medical care. Psychoactive medication can be an appropriate form of intervention. Thankfully, the stigma of consulting a psychiatrist is fading away, and in the past fifteen years the advances in anxiety and depression medication have been outstanding.

Antidepressants and related medications may be needed as part of an overall strategy to deal with anxiety and depression. And Christians are using these medications (even Christian leaders I know) with good results. The Bible recommends the appropriate use of drugs for medicinal purposes (see 1 Timothy 5:23), including the treatment of anxiety and depression due to hardship and trouble (see Proverbs 31:6-7; compare Job 29:13). I found treatment with antidepressants to be of great value for my own condition.

If we turn to psychoactive medications are we not trusting God? No more than if we turn to aspirin, antibiotics, or other medications. Consider that God has intervened at crucial moments in the history of medicine, frequently guiding medical researchers in their discoveries, even without their knowing it or without their being believers (see John 11:49-52). God is not only active in the spiritual salvation of people, He's also interested in other matters of our lives and has created many basic ingredients within His creation that can be used for our physical health. For example, the heart medicine digitalis comes from a very common flower called foxglove. Of course, medications should never become substitutes for seeking divine healing in a more direct, miraculous way. But properly understood, *both* miraculous healing and medicines are from God. If we can take medication for a stomachache, why not take medication for a brain-chemistry dysfunction? Depression and anxiety-related symptoms are treatable conditions, especially when part of a holistic approach.

Of course, medications are not the sole tools to be used in defeating anxiety and depression, but they can be an aid to help the brain function more normally while we then face the important spiritual and psychological issues.

PSYCHOLOGICAL ASPECTS OF ANXIETY AND DEPRESSION

Psychological intervention is a crucial component of an effective strategy for addressing anxiety and depression. There is considerable biblical support for the usefulness of psychological help that does not derive its insight specifically from the Bible, although such insight should never contradict the Bible. The Bible actually praises the ethical, life-related wisdom of unbelievers (see 1 Kings 4:29-34) and it acknowledges that all humans have access to God's moral law revealed in nature, irrespective of whether or not they have access to Holy Scripture (see Amos 1–2; Romans 1–2).[5] Scripture also teaches that we can gain valuable psychological insights and life-related lessons by watching biological creatures such as ants (see Proverbs 6:6-11), by studying natural phenomena such as rain (see Matthew 5:45), and by observing the behavior and social roles of others (see Proverbs 7:6-27).

In my own journey through this dark valley, I sought out a wise, trained, Christian counselor-therapist. Of course, that therapists are also Christian believers does not guarantee that their psychological approach is completely true, and non-Christian therapists' approaches are not guaranteed to be totally false. Even a non-Christian therapist can, in principle, help someone with anxiety and depression, though care must be exercised in adopting the advice of such a therapist.

A good Christian therapist is an expert at spotting our tendencies to distort how we view life, because we are too close to the problem. We all have a tendency to suppress emotions and memories, to project our "stuff" onto others, and in various ways to avoid owning our own issues. A trained third party can bring to the surface the meaning of events or patterns of thought. He or she can probe the significance of feelings and behaviors in our current situation or in earlier stages of life. My Christian therapist not only helped me recognize and understand my tendency to feel responsible for and fix other people's problems but also showed me ways to replace those patterns with less destructive habits.

Therapeutic insights can be life changing as they help us keep functioning in life while we're in the midst of a significant period of anxiety and depression. In early sessions with my therapist, I learned that people tend to stop doing things that bring them satisfaction such as jogging, reading, or socializing in various ways. He helped me see the need to maintain a few meaningful activities which, if set aside, could actually worsen the depression. Obviously, there are two ends on a continuum—doing too much and doing too little—and I was guided with specific steps to find the proper balance for my situation.

One of the great benefits of a counseling relationship is the experience of a *safe* environment in which we can feel the acceptance of another person who's skilled at understanding life. The counselor's desire is to help us identify appropriate physical, emotional, and other boundaries for ourselves so that we may be restored to healthy functioning. Many times I left an appointment not so much with a new insight as with an emotional experience that helped to restore some sense of my old feelings of well-being and wholeness.

THE SPIRITUAL SIDE OF ANXIETY AND DEPRESSION

Meditation is an important part of dealing with anxiety and depression. In chapter 4, we discussed the practice of memorizing and meditating on Scripture as a part of continuous prayer. But when we're in a troubled state, our brains may be too confused to do much memory work. So, meditating on a small number of favorite texts that help with anxiety and depression may be more helpful. Let the following comforting passages become the rails on which you run your life during a trying season of life.

A key passage many have found helpful is Paul wisely urging that "whatever is true, whatever is honorable, whatever is right, whatever is pure, whatever is lovely, whatever is of good repute, if there is any excellence and if anything worthy of praise, dwell on these things" (Philippians 4:8, NASB). There is great beauty in our world on which to meditate. Further, we can meditate on God's wonderful acts toward us and those for whom we care. Remembering times we received or gave of ourselves in love or extended forgiveness, times when the presence of God was especially precious, and answers to prayer (a topic we will return to later) — these are also proper objects for meditation.

When we're anxious and depressed, the so-called grand things of life may be too difficult to hold our attention. But anyone can start by being thankful for the sound of falling rain or the sight of ducks swimming in a pond or even the wonderful taste of a morning cup of coffee or a glass of orange juice.

THE HEART AND THE SCIENTIFIC ASPECT OF MEDITATION

The term *heart* has many uses in Scripture, but its basic meaning refers to the deepest core of the person. The heart is the fundamental, sometimes hidden fountain at the deepest recesses of a person. It is the absolute center from which spring our feelings, our most authentic thoughts, our values, our "take on life." In this sense, the heart is the deepest aspect of our soul, our inner self, and it is not to be equated with the organ that pumps blood.

It is no accident that the term *heart* is used to represent our deepest core. The physical heart area—what C. S. Lewis called "the chest"—is where we actually experience our deepest values, feelings, attitudes, and ways of seeing the world. In some mysterious way, then, the *physical* heart area is also our *metaphorical* heart. It's the center of meditation from which flow the feelings and imaginings of our deepest core.

A scientific strand of thought derived from recent discoveries may shed further light on biblical teaching about the core of a person related to the heart organ.[6] Neuroscientists have discovered that the heart has its own independent nervous system, referred to as "the brain in the heart." Truly, the heart thinks for itself. Some forty thousand neurons exist in the heart, which is as many as are found in several important subregions of the brain.

The heart sends signals to different parts of the brain, including the amygdala. The amygdala specializes in strong emotional memories. By influencing it and other regions of the brain, scientists have come to believe that "our heartbeats are not just the mechanical throbs of a diligent pump, but an *intelligent language* that significantly influences how we perceive and react to the world."[7] Some scientists talk about "heart intelligence," an intelligent flow of awareness and insight, an intuitive source of wisdom and clear perception that embraces both mental and emotional intelligence.

In biblical terms, the soul is the person. But the soul has two faculties—intellectual cognition and intuitive perception—and each is associated with a different body part—the brain and the heart, respectively. Thus the brain and the heart work together to shape our thoughts, emotions, moods, and attitudes. Given that a person is just one self with one soul, it is apparent that the "I," the soul, uses both the mind (associated with the brain) and the deepest intuitive core (associated with the heart organ) to think, see, and feel about the world.

We can marvel at the incredible accuracy of Paul's statement, "Be anxious for nothing, but in everything by prayer and supplication with thanksgiving let your requests be made known to God. And the peace of God, which surpasses all comprehension, will guard your *hearts and your minds* in Christ Jesus" (Philippians 4:6-7, NASB, emphasis added). Notice that the context is the feeling of anxiety. So, both the heart and the mind (the heart organ and the brain) must be involved cooperatively in opening up to God and dispelling anxiety.

The scientific findings suggest a practical meditation technique for handling anxiety and depression, which we'll discuss in the following pages. This was first presented by stress researcher Dr. Doc Childre, but we've adapted it to take into account biblical teaching.[8]

When we are anxious or depressed, we tend to obsess in cyclical thinking, to think over and over again about certain fearful or hurtful thoughts. We do this to try to anticipate a bad or worst-case scenario and to reassure ourselves that we are safe, that we can handle it. We also relive or replay in our minds traumatic events and their associated thoughts and emotions. Sometimes we center on a "safe" thought or emotion—one that we can handle. Because we can't face all of our fears and worries, we project all of them onto one or two issues that are "safer" for us to dwell on.

The problem with this strategy is that we get into a rut that is increasingly hard to escape from. As we mentioned earlier, studies have shown that obsessive thought and emotional patterns, as well as behaviors, literally create a neural pathway, a groove in the brain, that becomes habitual and contributes to a situation in which a person is literally stuck on a pattern, stuck in a rut.

Among other things, this means that trying to battle anxiety and depression in the head by obsessively worrying is a losing battle. We try to keep from repetitively entertaining the worry, but we have to exert increasing energy inwardly just to suppress the worry. This can deplete the brain of needed chemicals and lead to further depression.

Four Meditative Steps to Attend to Our Heart

Rather than encouraging you to battle anxiety and depression in the head, we recommend a four-step meditative strategy to deal with it in the heart. This form of meditation is a life-enhancing strategy even if you don't have anxiety or depression. But it is especially useful during a season of mental suffering.

Step 1: When obsessing on an anxious thought or stressful feeling, freeze-frame it. Take a time-out. If you have an anxious thought or stressful feeling right now, recognize it and bring it before your mind. Suppose it is the fear of financial ruin. As this thought and its associated emotion run over and over again in your awareness, freeze it. That is, stop your mental engine from running over and over again, and as you would stop a film projector, stop in midthought and freeze it. Step 1 helps a person to obey the biblical injunction to "cease striving" and stop fretting (Psalm 46:10, NASB; see Philippians 4:6).

Step 2: With all your might, shift your focus away from your racing mind or troublesome emotions and focus the center of your attention on your physical heart muscle. Attend to the center of your chest, where your heart is, and stay there for ten to fifteen seconds. The goal is to feel the area around your heart.

There are two ways to help you in this. First, pretend you are breathing in and out of your heart muscle. Second, try to "feel" and attend to the front surface of your physical heart, then the back surface, followed by the right then the left side. When first learning to practice this meditative activity and form it as a habit, you should take as long as necessary to focus on the heart area. At this point you may feel little emotion there, or you may get in touch with a feeling of embarrassment, fear, grief, sadness, loneliness, helplessness, hurt, or some other anxiety producer.

Step 2 is an aid in internalizing Proverbs 3:5: "Trust in the Lord with all your heart and lean not on your own understanding." Rather than mulling your worries over and over again in your mind and trying to solve them in the head, turn to the core of your inner life, your heart, and learn to trust God there.

Step 3: Using the acrostic CFAN, recall a memory emotion associated with the relevant memory and let that emotion dwell in and dominate the heart area. With your attention on your physical heart area, work to bring a new positive emotion, a healthy intuitive awareness, to dwell there and replace the feelings already there from the worrisome thought you have frozen. To do this, meditate on something positive in order to recall a memory emotion that is positive.

CFAN stands for Compassion, Forgiveness, Appreciation, and Nonjudgmentalism. You want to recall a specific occasion that you can picture in which you either gave or received compassion/love, forgiveness/removal of guilt feelings, appreciation/joy, or nonjudgmental attitude/acceptance.

You may not want to try all four of these (CFAN) at once, but pick one that is most effective for you and constantly return there. For example, recall a time when you gave real love to God, a friend, or a family member or received the feeling of love from God or someone important to you. Recall a time when you gave appreciation to someone or a special time of worship when you really felt God was there or perhaps a time when you gave heartfelt praise and adoration to someone. Or even recall a time when you drank in appreciation—from savoring the taste of coffee to receiving a spectacular answer to prayer or an endearing biblical truth. And so on. The goal here is not simply to recall the relevant incident, but more important, also to have the associated emotion fill and remain in your heart area.

Step 4: While holding this emotion in your physical heart area, return to the anxious thought and melt it piece by piece into the heart area and, with full sincerity, ask your heart, "Next time, what would be a less stressful, less anxious, more effective response to this thought and the situation to which it refers?" Listen to the heart area for an answer. The goal of step 4 is to so trust in the Lord with your whole heart that you form the habit of responding there to a worry with compassion, forgiveness, appreciation, and a nonjudgmental attitude toward yourself or others.

Here's how to break the worrisome thing down into pieces and melt it into the heart. Take the thought—for example, *I am going to be ruined financially*—and break it down to its parts (my children will be embarrassed at school by their clothes; I will be out of a job; my family will look down on me). By taking that part to the heart area, you can allow the anxious thought to be overwhelmed by and newly associated with a positive emotion instead of negative ones. If you do this at various times each day, a habit will form that will allow you to set the thought aside and not get stuck on it. You can learn to have the thought while feeling, say, joy and compassion.

ADJUSTING OUR BELIEFS AND STRETCHING OUR FAITH

During my period of anxiety and depression, I felt helpless and hopeless. Clearly, I needed hope. I needed to feel that Someone was there who could and would catch me. I needed to know that there is a supernatural God who still answers specific prayers, who still heals and speaks to His children in miraculous ways, who intervenes as He did with the people in biblical times. I needed to feel and really, really believe in a God who shows up.

Maybe it was my immaturity, maybe it was my desperation, but a God who "merely" revealed timeless wisdom to me in His book and who did something long ago to save me from hell was just not enough for me. Perhaps it should have been, but I needed an "Abba" who was watching over me intently and who would step in at crucial moments to rescue me from my own wickedness and those who would harm me, both human and demonic. That's the sort of God the psalms talk about and that was the sort of God for whom I deeply hungered.

What an anxious and depressed person needs is to really believe that the kinds of experiences and divine encounters that took place with folks in biblical times also take place now—that, in fact, they could really happen to him or her. Such a genuine hope can be life-sustaining in hard times. Here's what I recommend from my own experience.

MEDITATE ON GOD'S PAST ACTIONS IN YOUR LIFE

The first thing to think about is your own story, that is, specific answers to prayer or other sorts of healings that have happened in your life. If you do this, it will strengthen your faith incredibly. In my case, I recalled a time in June 2003 during the early stage of my depression when I had a miraculous answer to prayer. It helped to sustain me during the next several months as I kept it before my mind.

On a Tuesday morning early in June, I went for an eight o'clock jog. During the run I decided to take time to walk and pray. I told the Lord that I was at a point where I really needed to see Him intervene for me. Suddenly, a thought came to my mind from "nowhere," saying, "Why don't you ask Me to do something for you now?" I wasn't sure it was the Lord or my own thoughts, though it did have a feeling I have come to recognize as a signal that God is speaking to me. Because of my family's financial need, I asked the Lord to bring us five thousand dollars that day. I returned home, showered, and went about my day as best I could, given my anxiety and depression. My faith was not particularly strong at the time. The mail came and went with no check. But at 5:40 that evening, completely unexpectedly, I received five thousand dollars from someone who knew me but knew nothing of my situation. It was simply incredible, and my entire family fell to its knees in worship.

Later that summer, I was in the middle of a five-day lecture series in Columbia, South Carolina. As I previously mentioned, my depression made me feel that all the academic work I had done over the years for the cause of Christ—especially my intellectual writings produced to defend the faith—were worthless and a complete waste of time. Even more destructively, I felt my life was basically meaningless.

Just before dinner on July 15, I started getting an extreme migraine headache. Now, I can go five years without even a small headache, so this was a first for me. I took Tylenol, canceled my evening lecture, and went to bed in my dorm room at the school. But things got worse. My head was racked with pain. Around six, I received a phone call from a conferee who lived in the area. He said he was taking me to the emergency room. I slumped into his front seat and he drove me to a walk-in clinic about twenty miles away. I staggered in, left my driver's license at the front desk, and was whisked away to the emergency room. Immediately, two nurses hooked monitors to my chest and brain, and began testing me. My blood pressure was off the charts. They gave me an injection to alleviate the headache, and it began to work quickly.

After about five minutes of this, the doctor on call that evening walked in the door. Holding my driver's license he said, "Are you J. P. Moreland? The one who teaches at Talbot Seminary?" Taken a bit off guard, I nodded. "I don't believe this!" he said. "If I could pick one person in the entire country to come in here it would be you. Dr. Moreland, I can't thank you enough for what you have done in the intellectual world for the cause of Christ. I have read almost all your books and, hey, you know that book *Body and Soul* you wrote with Scott Rae? I teach ethics at a local community college and I use that as a text. I can't believe I am getting to meet you!"

It turned out that I had most likely eaten some bad shrimp at dinner the day before (it takes about twenty-four hours for food poisoning to hit someone). But as soon as this doctor shared with me the impact I had had on him, the Lord spoke to me: "I am well-pleased with your academic work for My name's sake. You have done well. Keep trusting Me."

Beyond reasonable doubt, this was no coincidence. At the very moment of my need to be reassured of the meaning of my intellectual work, I met a doctor who "happened" to be on duty that evening in a city I'd never before visited, who valued the very work for which I needed consolation during my depression. Praise God for bad shrimp!

Meditating on things like this has reassured me that God knows about my anxiety and depression, and I can have legitimate hope that He hears my prayers and acts when the timing is right. I recommend that you record answers to your prayers and other miracles in a journal right after they happen. You don't have to do it daily. I don't. But after thirty years of journaling, I have hundreds of stories like the one I just mentioned. Our problem is not that God does not act on our behalf. Our problem is that, as time passes, we forget how needy we once were, and we forget the details, the drama, and the gratitude we experienced from answers to prayer.

MEDITATE ON GOD'S ACTIONS FOR OTHERS

Eighteen months ago, my friend Brian Slezak went to Northern California to teach pastors and laypeople how to pray for the sick. At the conference, a man came up to ask for prayer. A grenade had exploded near him in Vietnam, and he had been blind in one eye for three decades. Brian and a prayer team of two others sensed that the power of the Holy Spirit was present for healing. They calmly laid hands on the man and prayed. His eyesight was instantly restored! Brian and the others in the team have given testimony to this miracle, and they are trustworthy men. Meditating on this fact can create faith and expectation when one brings one's hardships before the Lord. It also creates hope because it reminds us that God is a living God who shows up to care for His children!

READ BOOKS RECOUNTING GOD'S MIRACLES

Finally, read and meditate on books and magazines (such as *Guideposts*) that tell authentic stories of signs and wonders by almighty God. I cannot tell you how much this sort of reading kept me going during the toughest point of my anxiety and depression.[9]

At the end of the day, our fundamental hope in suffering is best expressed by this simple yet profound prayer: "Turn to me and be gracious to me, for I am lonely and afflicted. The troubles of my heart are enlarged; bring me out of my distresses" (Psalm 25:16-17, NASB).

During my time of depression, not only did I receive crucial help from a competent Christian therapist, I also relied on close friends as never before. In the final chapter we highlight the importance of not taking this journey alone. [10]

QUESTIONS FOR PERSONAL REFLECTION
AND GROUP DISCUSSION

1. Give yourself permission now to move into a time of solitude and silence by reflecting and journaling on either of the following:

   a. Remembering past uplifting emotional experiences is one important means of sustaining a healthy emotional life, as discussed in chapter 3. Use the acrostic CFAN as a prod and recall a time when you experienced one of the following, either receiving it from someone or offering it to someone: compassion, forgiveness, appreciation, or nonjudgmental acceptance. Consider journaling your reflections on these to help you process them and to be able to reread your reflections at a later date.

   b. Meditate on God's miraculous and supernatural intervention in your life or in the life of someone else. When has God shown up in your life in such a way that you knew it was surely no coincidence? (Consider getting a copy of one of the books recommended in note 9 of this chapter as a means to strengthen your faith in our supernatural God.)

2. For believers who enter a time of depression and anxiety, the author proposes that we attend to all aspects of our human nature: the physical side with appropriate diet, exercise, and medication; the psychological side with wise counsel and

therapy; the spiritual side with meditative spiritual disciplines and healing prayer.

    a. Which of the various approaches to handling anxiety and depression make sense to you?

    b. Think through the issues: How would you defend the position that Christians should consider primarily "spiritual" resources in dealing with depression and anxiety and should avoid assistance from antidepressant medications or psychological counseling and therapy? How would you defend the position of using an approach involving appropriate assistance within all three arenas: medical, psychological, spiritual?

3. Try the spiritual discipline of attending to your physical heart as suggested in this chapter (pages 168–171). Reread the section slowly and ask God to guide you in this exercise. Identify something you are stressing over or worrying about and pause at each of the four steps. It may take going through the whole process a few times to get a feel for its desired effect.

CHAPTER EIGHT

CULTIVATING SPIRITUAL
FRIENDSHIPS

HOW CONNECTED WITH OTHERS ARE YOU ON LIFE'S JOURNEY? DO you have close friendships? I (Klaus) ask this question not to make you feel uncomfortable, but out of a sense of urgency. We *can't* walk through this life alone. I'm not saying we *shouldn't* do it alone. I mean that it's not even possible to walk with God in the depths that He desires to open up to us if we try to do it on our own. Further, without a friend who knows us well—someone close enough to know our struggles and our pain—we are in danger of many temptations. We need one or more friends, not just to turn to when life gets tough, but as companions who can encourage us regularly.

I should know. I'm a recovering loner. And it's still not fully out of my system. Go-it-alone assumptions, acquired over a lifetime of living in this fallen world, continue to compel me *not* to rely on others. I'd rather do it myself, thank you.

Can you picture a castle with a moat and the drawbridge raised? Surrounding the moat is a town with houses and businesses. Perhaps this image will give you an idea of the state of my inner life regarding relationships. The castle was mine, but I also had a house outside the castle. In town I would visit with people and engage in work and ministry, a normal kind of involvement in life. But no one really was invited into my castle, because it was hard for me to trust anyone else.

It has been only within the past few years that I have begun to lower that drawbridge and allow a few people to enter inside. As I have let my defenses down with these few, God has begun to touch my soul in new places, to help me feel both deep joy and deep sorrow—wells of emotion that were always there, unknown to me. And I have grown much closer to God as I have grown closer to my friends.

I came to a point that I realized a haunting truth: If I can't depend on a few trusted others whom I can see, what makes me so sure that I can really rely on God, whom I can't see? Might an adaptation of 1 John 4:20 fit here?: "If we say we depend on God yet can't depend on a fellow believer, we are liars." Lately, I've seen that life is a school for learning how to have faith in others and not to depend on ourselves alone. God actually made us to function and flourish by mutual dependence on spiritual friends. From early on, our experiences can help us learn how to depend on others, to grow our "trust" muscles—ultimately, so we can deepen our trust and reliance on God. I've discovered that we desperately need to be connected to a group of close friends if we want to deepen our trust in God.

IN THE COMPANY OF GOD

The model for our relationships is our triune God himself. Although God is one divine Being, He is not one person. The Bible teaches that God is an eternally existing fellowship or friendship of three persons (see, for example, Isaiah 48:16; 61:1; Matthew 28:19; 2 Corinthians 13:14). As theologian J. I. Packer phrased it, "The one God ('he') is also, and equally, 'they,' and 'they' are always together and always cooperating."[1]

Scripture also affirms the deity of each person: Father (John 6:27), Son (Hebrews 1:8), and Holy Spirit (Acts 5:3-4) and records statements by each person using the personal pronoun *I* (Father: "I am well pleased," 2 Peter 1:17; Son: "I am Jesus," Acts 9:5; Holy Spirit: "I have sent them," Acts 10:20). Yet God is still *one* (James 2:19), manifesting the ideal unity and harmony of wills along with a unique unity of divine essence.

Isn't it amazing that God is an eternally existing "divine society" of three persons who love each other maximally and who comprise the one Christian God? Furthermore, the love each person of the Godhead has for the other persons is the benchmark for all loving relationships, giving us a living model of the value of community and friendship among believers.

In His prayer for us as His future disciples, Jesus invites us to experience a similar kind of oneness with each other and with the three persons of the Godhead. Count the number of times the preposition *in* occurs in this passage. Also note the unusual use of the pronouns for God (*we* and *us*).

> ". . . that all of them [that's us, His future disciples] may be one, Father, just as you are *in* me and I am *in* you. May they also be *in us* so that the world may believe that you have sent me. I have given them the glory that you gave me, that they may be one as *we* are one: I *in* them and you *in* me. May they

be brought to complete unity to let the world know that you
sent me and have loved them even as you have loved me."
(John 17:21-23, emphasis added)

As an eternal fellowship of three divine persons, our God is characterized by a robust interdependence through the mutual indwelling of each person within the Trinity. The technical term for this mutual indwelling is *perichoresis* (pronounced parry-co-reesis). This truth is based on John 17:21: "as you are *in* me and I am *in* you" (emphasis added). Amazingly, we are invited into that fellowship "that all of them may be one, Father, just as you are in me and I am in you. May they also be in us." The love relationships within the Trinity set the tone and benchmark for all our relationships, for "God is love" (1 John 4:8).

If we pattern our lives after the Trinity, we come to a startling conclusion: We are individuals who exist for and flourish best in community with others. Also, the ideal community nurtures and respects the individuality of each of its members. Such an ideal community is best achieved among close spiritual friends. But for those of us shaped by the values of contemporary Western culture, unhealthy independence is a serious threat to our ability to find and cultivate such close friendships.

HOW DOES A CLOSE FRIENDSHIP FEEL?

I've had various relationships over the years, but one stands out. In fact, this book in your hands is one result of my growing and deepening friendship with J. P. Moreland. I can honestly say that

God has uniquely used J. P. to call me to become more of the person God designed me to be and to draw me much closer to God. I feel safe in J. P.'s presence. I sense down deep that he is on my side. He wants my best. He wants me to succeed. He often offers an encouraging word that buoys me. At the same time, he feels free to point out a truth that may hurt or embarrass me.

Consider two events that illustrate this, one in which J. P. was by my side, another in which he was in my face. Without letting me know, he graciously attended a professional conference session where I presented a paper that launched me into new arenas of research. Just before the session was to begin, I felt overwhelmed and wondered why I had requested to give this paper. Who was *I* to offer a new perspective on this matter? The small room was packed with attendees also interested in the topic. And J. P. was sitting up front. He was there to bail me out in case I faltered during the question time. Just before the session began, he came up to me, assured me of his affection, and promised to be there for me. What a comfort and encouragement!

J. P. is also willing to take risks in a relationship, to do the hard thing if good could result. One time he sat me down and invaded the privacy of my finances. Among the areas of his strength, J. P. is good at the discipline of finances. I felt very uncomfortable. I had made some unwise financial decisions, and just having that conversation brought up the embarrassment of those decisions, which were limiting my situation at the time. Kindly and openly, as only a close friend can, J. P. asked a few penetrating questions. Then he brainstormed with me some practical ideas to work toward a specific financial goal over the next two years. At the time, he used one of his pet phrases: "Go to school on me on this." With some discipline and God's kindness, Beth and I achieved that financial goal, something we thought was beyond our reach. A close friend had believed in us and had helped us move toward a goal, even in the private arena of finances.

The Bible provides some crucial insights about the varied characteristics of how close friends can relate to each other. Following is a list of verses in the New Testament that include the phrase "one another" or something like it, such as "encourage one another" (emphasis has been added in each). Of course, each verse must be studied in its own context to appreciate the full meaning. But this quick reference guide gives us a fairly complete picture of the breadth and depth for what close friendships can look like:

- *Accept* one another. (Romans 15:7)
- *Admonish* one another. (Colossians 3:16; Romans 15:14)
- Do what leads to peace and *building up* of one another. (Romans 14:19)
- *Carry* each other's burdens. (Galatians 6:2)
- Have equal *concern* for each another. (1 Corinthians 12:25)
- *Confess* your sins to each other. (James 5:16)
- *Be devoted* to one another. (Romans 12:10)
- *Encourage* one another. (1 Thessalonians 4:18; Hebrews 3:13; 10:25)

- *Bear with* one another. (Ephesians 4:2; Colossians 3:13)
- *Forgive* one another. (Ephesians 4:32; Colossians 3:13)
- *Greet* one another with a holy kiss. (Romans 16:16; 2 Corinthians 13:12)
- *Don't grumble* against each other. (James 5:9)
- *Honor* one another. (Romans 12:10)
- Offer *hospitality* to one another. (1 Peter 4:9)
- Clothe yourselves with *humility* toward one another. (1 Peter 5:5)
- Be *kind* and compassionate to one another. (Ephesians 4:32)
- Do not *lie* to each other. (Colossians 3:9)
- Be *patient,* bearing with one another. (Ephesians 4:2; Colossians 3:12-13)
- Live in *peace* with each other. (1 Thessalonians 5:13)
- *Pray* for each other. (James 5:16)
- Live in harmony and be of the *same mind* toward one another. (Romans 12:16; 15:5; Philippians 2:2, NASB)
- *Serve* one another in love. (Galatians 5:13; 1 Peter 4:10)
- Do not *slander* one another. (James 4:11)
- *Speak* to one another with psalms, hymns, and spiritual songs. (Ephesians 5:19)
- *Speak truth* each one of you with his neighbor. (Ephesians 4:25, NASB)
- *Spur* one another on toward love and good deeds. (Hebrews 10:24)
- *Submit* to one another. (Ephesians 5:21)

- *Teach* one another. (Colossians 3:16, NASB)
- *Wait* for one another. (1 Corinthians 11:33, NASB)

Notice that some of these friendship qualities can be experienced at almost any level of relationship, such as "greet one another" or "offer hospitality to one another." Yet others on the list require a greater depth of trust and intimacy to be experienced in their fullest expression. Some of these deeper ones are "admonish one another," "confess your sins to each other," and "submit to one another."

This list of "one another" verses can become a supportive guide to help us identify specific areas that need to be explored if we wish to deepen our existing friendships. We have lost something in the church when we are interested only in making others like us and are afraid to risk.

Did Jesus cultivate and honor friendships? Sometimes He seemed distant and even condemning of close relationships. Consider Matthew 5:46-47: "If you love those who love you, what reward will you get? Are not even the tax collectors doing that? And if you greet only your brothers, what are you doing more than others? Do not even pagans do that?"

We must look at Jesus' own practice to understand His perspective on friendships. In His role as head of the church, Jesus invited twelve people to spend a few years in daily living together. These disciples, also called apostles, became the foundational leaders of the church. Occasionally, Jesus took with Him only an inner circle of close friends: Peter, James, and John, for example, at the raising of Jairus's daughter (see Mark 5:37), at Jesus' transfiguration (see 9:2), and in His most difficult time of testing in Gethsemane, when He needed His friends to pray for Him (see 14:33). Among these, John became His closest friend, known as the one "whom Jesus loved" (John 13:23; 21:7,20; 19:26; 20:2). The gospel of John also records that "Jesus loved Martha and her sister and Lazarus" (11:5). When Jesus passed through Bethany near Jerusalem, He often stayed with the sisters and their brother, the one whom Jesus eventually raised from the dead.

In light of Jesus' own practice of having friends, He doesn't prohibit friendship love in Matthew 5. Rather He condemns only an *exclusive* focus on friendship love as the totality of our sphere of relationships. As we cultivate deeper friendships, we can expand our range of hospitality and generosity beyond these friends to those who may be unlovable or who can't always repay our love.

FRIENDS AND NEIGHBORS

Unfortunately, we make the word *friend* cover too much territory—from best friends to people we hardly know. Most of our relationships are happenstance arrangements that fit under the biblical term *neighbor*: the person (or *boor*—literally, *peasant*) who happens to be near (*nigh*). These include people at work, at school, at church, and even our family and extended relations. They are near us in some way (geographically, or figuratively speaking with family blood or marriage ties). For all these, Jesus calls us to show and share Christian love.

Furthermore, within our church and beyond, we mentor and meet the needs of various ones God has brought near to us. We use our gifts and resources to minister in love to brothers and sisters in

Christ (see Galatians 5:13). We are called to warmly care for these dear brothers and sisters, even though we don't necessarily embrace them as bosom buddies or close friends.

Close friends are people we choose to invite into our hearts in a special way. Through many and varied shared experiences over time, we grow to mutually enjoy each other's company, no matter the circumstance or hardship. Perhaps it's because we already have a deep love for our friends that Jesus needed to exhort us to love our "neighbor" (Matthew 22:39; Luke 10:27; Romans 13:9; Galatians 5:14; James 2:8) and not our friends only (see Matthew 5:46; Luke 14:12).

Yet even among those we call friends, there are differences. I've found that a classical threefold typology devised by Aristotle, the ancient Greek philosopher, offers help in this. Consider what it is that attracts us to another person. One of Aristotle's categories involves relationships that are based on the enjoyment of *common interest, values, or pleasures,* such as golf partners, members of a quilting club, or a group that gets together Saturday evening for a game or other recreation. Most of our Christian friends or church members might also be included in this category, because the association is based on a common interest in loving and serving God.

Another form of attraction in our relationships comes from *benefits or advantages* that may come to us. We may call this a relationship of "helpfulness" or "usefulness." The benefit may result from skills the person has — for example, a business partner who does well at sales or a teammate in a soccer club who plays his position well. People who serve together in a ministry tend to bring different talents and gifts through which God effects change in lives. Of course, ministry team members also share common values. We may also barter benefits with our own resources: trading days off or using a friend's pickup truck or specialty gardening tool.

These two categories of relationships—one of shared interests and the other of mutual benefits—are common. Most of our current relationships began in some way through these general entry points. Think about your own close friendships. Can you recall how each one developed? You'll probably see one or both of these factors involved.

But there is a third category that moves beyond these initial points of contact and, with a few people, can grow into close friendship relationships. In Aristotle's final category, people seek the friendship for its own sake, what may be called *a friendship of character*. In this kind of relationship, we seek to be with a person for the sake of the friend himself or herself, not solely for common interests or for benefits to be received, although that's how the relationship may have first developed. Mysteriously at times, what blossoms with a few people is a full-flowered friendship of character in which close friends appreciate each other for who they are and seek to help each other grow in a life of goodness, truth, and beauty. Such a relationship nourishes a deep and mutual love that characterizes this third category.

One way to summarize these points about differences in our relationships could be the following image. Picture in your mind three concentric circles to represent all of our relationships, from a small circle in the middle to larger ones as they move away from the center. The central circle represents our close and best friends—what Aristotle called friendships of character. Here a genuine mutuality exists, one for the other. We seek to be with these special ones primarily for their own sake, not for other reasons. We carry these few in our heart throughout the day, and with these we tend to socialize and connect most often. The next circle is a bit larger and includes friends with whom we share interests and values as well as those friendships involving some exchange of benefits and skills. The largest circle encompasses the rest of our relationships, those people with whom we have some type of regular contact.

DEVELOPING CLOSE RELATIONSHIPS

We've already looked at various Scripture passages that relate to friendship (for example, the "one another" passages). For some guidance on the how-tos of developing closer friendships, we'll draw on some practical wisdom from the past, a classical discussion of friendship from the Middle Ages: *Spiritual Friendship* by Aelred of Rievaulx (AD 1110–1167). As an abbot of a monastery, Aelred was responsible for the development of community among the brothers. From his knowledge of Scripture and years of experience, he offered his insights in the form of conversations on the topic with various brothers at the abbey. Of course, the basis of the closest friendships is that both persons are genuine Christians, being formed by and formed into the love of God in Christ. Aelred explained that the qualities of intimate friendships "take their beginning from Christ, advance through Christ, and are perfected in Christ."[2]

Aelred pointed out that, this side of heaven, not everyone will be the best match as close friends. Before welcoming another into a deep and mutual commitment of close friendship, Aelred advised that we look for evidence of the characteristics important for good friendships. He proposed a process of getting to know people who might become our best friends, a process somewhat comparable to our contemporary dating and courtship practices that can lead to marriage.

But why all this bother? Don't friendships just happen? Can we really have any part in their cultivation? In one sense, it is true that close friendships are good gifts from God. But it's also true that we have a part to play. Based on years of empirical research, University of Chicago professor Mihaly Csikszentmihalyi critiqued the myth that friendships just seem to come about naturally:

> Just as with the family, people believe that friendships happen naturally, and if they fail, there is nothing to be done about it but feel sorry for yourself. In adolescence, when so many interests are shared with others and one has great stretches of free time to invest in a relationship, making friends might seem like a spontaneous process. But later in life friendships rarely happen by chance: one must cultivate them as assiduously as one must cultivate a job or a family.[3]

Isn't it the case that all valuable things in life require some participation on our part? Surely this includes friendships as well. Even the book of Proverbs warns us about associating too closely with persons with certain vices, so that we don't become like them (for example, Proverbs 22:24-25; 23:20; 24:1). When we do have a choice about the people we'd like to have in our innermost circle of close friends, we need to decide carefully with wisdom.

But before we move too far into this discussion, we first need to look in the mirror at ourselves. Do I assume I'm already a great catch as a good friend? Am I a person who epitomizes fully the lofty qualities discussed on the following pages? Not only can we assess qualities in others, but we must also ask, *How "friendly" am I?* As we consider the matter and consider our current relationships, we must include ourselves in the mix. To what extent do we have the qualities of a good friend?

CHARACTERISTICS OF A GOOD FRIENDSHIP

Let's be honest. There are some brothers and sisters in Christ who are difficult to be around. Some still have a long way to grow in their character. But, more importantly, we need to see our own blind spots. It is helpful to get honest feedback from a few mature Christian people we know, asking them, "How do I come across to others? Do people tend to think I am a difficult person to be around?" Jesus informed us that it's much easier to see the faults ("the speck") in others than in ourselves ("the log," Matthew 7:3, NASB).

We must give Christian kindness to all people, even the difficult. Yet we have no obligation to sustain a close friendship with Christians who manifest abusive traits or who are unable to engage in a mutually enriching, intimate adult relationship. Of course, we can minister to and extend Christian grace to our brothers and sisters represented in the outer circles of our relationships. But we must recognize a basic distinction between the open practice of Christian love to all and the special love for a close friend, Aelred explained:

> There is a vast difference; for divine authority approves that more are to be received into the bosom of charity [Christian love] than into the embrace of friendship. For we are compelled by the law of charity to receive in the embrace of [Christian] love not only our friends but also our enemies. But only those do we call friends to whom we can fearlessly entrust our heart and all its secrets; those, too, who, in turn, are bound to us by the same law of faith and security.[4]

Due to our personal and deep commitment to them, our close friends will receive a greater amount of our love, our time, and our trust.

Aelred identified four essential friendly characteristics we can acquire in ourselves and can find in those who might become our close friends: love, affection, security, and what might be called a caring openness and sharing with each other. To love means that we always seek what is best for the other person. Even in my fifties, I'm finding pockets of selfishness in how I relate to my wife. I'd rather use extra funds to buy books than to make our home more aesthetically pleasing. I want to spend my time doing what's fun for me and I don't always try to care for Beth's needs. I'm finding that as I attend more to her needs, I'm becoming a person she enjoys being around, which leads us to Aelred's next point.

Affection, displayed in our outward demeanor, signifies our inward pleasure with a friend. In the past five years or so, as Beth

194 ⟣ THE LOST VIRTUE OF HAPPINESS

and I have been growing in our companionship, we have had to
work at stopping what we called being "prickly" with each other.
With the baggage of two decades of marriage behind us, we
realized it wasn't always fun to be together. In God's grace, through
a variety of means, Beth and I began working toward becoming
friends again. Sometimes we bumped into each other's prickles
and hurt each other. Yet we persisted at seeking the good for each
other. Finally, on Valentine's Day 2003, Beth and I realized we again
had warm places in our hearts for each other. We carry each other
in our thoughts while apart and long to get back together again.
Close friends don't need reasons to be together. Being in each
other's presence is a joy in itself because it's a place of comfort and
transparency; we feel secure.

In exploring the concept of security, Aelred underlined the
importance of freely disclosing to each other the secrets of our
hearts without fear or suspicion. In a word, close friends are safe
to be around. There's no concern about cheap sarcasm at your
expense or a holier-than-thou spirit or a feeling of being invisible
while the other talks on and on about himself or herself. Close
friends listen to each other with a warm heart and they reverence
each other's intimate secrets. In our friend's presence, we're
entering a safety zone in which we can bare our souls and receive
comfort and care.

Finally, close friends experience "a pleasing and friendly sharing
of all events which occur, whether joyful or sad, of all thoughts,
whether harmful or useful, of everything taught or learned."[5] How
do we go about developing this kind of healthy dynamic? Part of

it comes by working courageously through our own harmful and selfish baggage (as we discussed in chapter 3). The kind of person I had become actually prevented me from entering into and fully enjoying a mutually fulfilling, deep friendship. It was worth the pain and effort to grow up in this area so I could become a better friend.

VICES THAT DIVIDE

What vices in those we might want to get to know as close friends does Aelred tell us to steer away from? Here are a few: being easily provoked to anger, being irresponsible and unstable, being suspicious and distrustful, and being overly talkative. Of course, our first consideration is to examine our own heart in these areas. We may gain some insight about hesitations others have about developing a deep friendship with us.

In the Sermon on the Mount, Jesus identified sinful anger at the top of His list of vices (see Matthew 5:21-26). As Dallas Willard notes, "It is the elimination of anger and contempt that [Jesus] presents as the first and fundamental step toward the rightness of the kingdom heart."[6] The wisdom of the Old Testament weighs in here as well: "Do not make friends with a hot-tempered man, do not associate with one easily angered" (Proverbs 22:24) and "Do not be quickly provoked in your spirit, for anger resides in the lap of fools" (Ecclesiastes 7:9).

Beyond these basics, Aelred also suggested that we be on the alert for certain destructive characteristics that cut short a budding friendship: a person lacking humility (for example, preferring praise and not freely giving any; unwillingness to admit wrong) and those with an undisciplined tongue (that is, slandering you in public; disclosing your secrets and confidences to others, talking in derogatory ways about you behind your back). We may also have to part ways with a friend when he or she intentionally harms or slanders a loved one or one to whom we're bound by loyalty or responsibility.

All of our relationships are windows to our soul. They give evidence for how our relationship with God is growing within us and how His love is moving through us to others. Learning how to love the unlovable is possible when we have some close friends. Our close friendships can become God's School of Love. Within such a safe context, we can try out how to incorporate all of the "one another" passages into our lifestyle, first within a friendship circle and then beyond. Then we can better reach out to others with God's love, for we can't give out what we don't experience ourselves. Close friendships offer the opportunity for making all of the aspects of healthy and mature community, described by the "one another" verses, a regular experience.

SOME PRACTICAL STEPS FORWARD

Perhaps a good place to start is by reflecting on your current friendships. Take the following CFQ—Close Friendship Quotient— and invite God to offer guidance in which areas mentioned in this chapter He might have you emphasize.

1. Three activities I especially enjoy doing with my close friends:
    a.
    b.
    c.

2. My close friendships give me satisfaction in these three significant ways:
    a.
    b.
    c.

3. Three important qualities that I bring to my close friendships:
    a.
    b.
    c.

4. I probably could improve my close friendships in these three important areas:
    a.
    b.
    c.

5. My close friendships really challenge me spiritually in a positive way.

    Strongly Agree   Strongly Disagree
            1   2   3   4   5   6

6. At this point in my life I am very satisfied with my close friendships.

Strongly Agree   Strongly Disagree

    1   2   3   4   5   6

Paul exhorts us, "Pursue righteousness, faith, love and peace, along with those who call on the Lord out of a pure heart" (2 Timothy 2:22). Perhaps you sense a readiness to move into deeper levels of closeness with one or more of your existing Christian friends. Here are suggestions of activities you can do together:

- Seek God together in prayer.
- Study God's Word together.
- Discuss personal aspirations.
- Reveal frustrations and hurts.
- Confess sins to each other.
- Serve God together.
- Socialize together.

Beyond this more personal forum, becoming regularly involved in a growing and relationally healthy small group of Christians is of utmost importance. Various avenues are available in your church and other Christian organizations or ministries to join together with other believers, perhaps with a study group, a support group, or a ministry team. Serving alongside believers provides opportunities to become acquainted with like-minded people who could eventually become close friends.

It's wise to seek various ways to grow in our relational and emotional maturity. For example, you may want to attend a marriage conference, enroll in a class on interpersonal communication and small-group dynamics, or read articles and books on the topics of community and friendship.[7] I also recommend that you consider regularly visiting with a mature Christian leader for guidance and personal feedback. My monthly meetings with a mentor have had a profound influence on my walk with God and my relationships with other people. Furthermore, you may wish to make an appointment with a Christian therapist for a psychological checkup and conversation about your relationships.

We also must notice where relationships have gone sour, for as the apostle John taught, "If we say we love God, yet hate a fellow believer, his brother, we are liars. For if we do not love a brother or sister, whom we have seen, we cannot love God, whom we have not seen. And he has given us this command: Those who love God must also love one another" (1 John 4:20-21, TNIV).

In his book *Power Healing*, John Wimber shared the story of a woman in her forties who had asked him to pray for healing of chronic stomach disorders and arthritis.[8] As Wimber prayed, he sensed that her bitterness was the root of the problem, particularly related to her sister. In response to his question about feeling any hostility, anger, or bitterness toward her sister, the woman stiffened and, though she admitted not having seen her sister for sixteen years, she replied in the negative. Wimber pressed further: "Are you sure?" The woman confessed that years earlier her sister had married a man she had loved and then had later divorced him. "I cannot forgive my sister for that."

"If you don't forgive her," Wimber told her, "your 'bones will waste away,'" as David had written in Psalm 32:3.

The woman relented and responded with concern, "What should I do?" Wimber suggested that she write a letter to her sister, forgiving her and also asking to renew their relationship. The woman did write the letter right away, but didn't mail it for several weeks. Yet her physical condition severely worsened to the point that she feared she might die. Suddenly, she was reminded of the letter to her sister. As she placed the letter into the mailbox, she began to experience relief and was completely healed when she arrived home.

We Can't Do It Alone

As I write these words, I have just returned from an unusual memorial service—not for a person, but for a building burned down during the Southern California fires of October and November 2003. It had been a site for personal renewal as a retreat center for pastors, missionaries, and students of spiritual formation. Judy and Gene Ten Elshof were called by God to raise up that place—a wonderful fifty-eight-acre site in the San Bernardino Mountains with a beautiful three-story home affording a grand view of the area. A stay at Hilltop had blessed many. But the fire eventually reached it and left little in its wake.

Those touched by Hilltop Renewal Ministries and those who knew the Ten Elshofs gathered for the memorial service. We mourned the loss, grieved with the Ten Elshofs, prayed for them, worshiped God, and asked Him to carry on His work through

Hilltop as the cleanup and plans for rebuilding commenced. After the moving service, I reflected on this unusual service with a friend. She said it was wonderful for the Ten Elshofs to have a community of saints to bear their burden and to come alongside during this difficult time. She said, "We can't do it alone."

When that time of crisis drops in on you—when you need someone's listening ear, comforting hug, or a place to stay overnight—to whom can you go? Who is that close friend who shares your heart, who would bend over backward to care for your soul, who loves as a close friend? The list on page 198 suggests a few of the things that good friends can do together, and books are suggested in the notes. What can you do today, this weekend, or this month to take some practical steps to deepen your friendships?

QUESTIONS FOR PERSONAL REFLECTION
OR GROUP DISCUSSION

1. Use the following prods to identify those within your circles of friendship, and list four or five names for each. (For the sake of this exercise, leave out names of family and mentors; focus on peer relationships.) With whom would you like to

   a. spend a fun day socially (for example, at a sports event, shopping, watching a movie, eating together)?

   b. serve on a ministry team or a short-term mission project?

   c. go to for comfort and help in an emergency?

   d. share a confidential prayer request?

   e. seek advice about an embarrassing sin habit?

   What insights do you gain about your peer relationships from the lists? And what insights did you gain from completing the Close Friendship Quotient exercise?

2. The foundational component for cultivating close Christian friendships is becoming a "friendly" person. Try one or more of the various suggestions in this chapter and focus on what is in your control: Ask a mentor for feedback on qualities you

CULTIVATING SPIRITUAL FRIENDSHIPS ❦ 203

have and areas to grow in; practice certain spiritual disciplines mentioned in the book (see especially chapter 3); take a class on interpersonal relationships and read a book on friendship; meet with a spiritual mentor monthly; or visit with a Christian psychologist for a psychological checkup about relationships.

3. Deepen your existing close friendships by using the list of "one another" verses (on pages 184–186) as a checklist assessing the quality and depth of each of your friendships. Use the list as a discussion starter: Which ones have you regularly practiced in a friendship in the past four to six weeks? For which "one another" is it time to begin moving into some new territory?

EPILOGUE

I WAS TEN MINUTES INTO AN EVANGELISTIC TALK TO SEVENTY college students when I (J. P.) noticed a straggler enter the back of the room. Curiously, he did not sit with the rest of the crowd, preferring to remain alone in a dim area near the back. I was about to find out why.

As the crowd began to disperse after my talk, I made a beeline to the back, hoping to catch the straggler before he could leave. As he was leaving the room, I beckoned, "Excuse me. What did you think of the talk?" I could see only his back, but I noticed that his clothes were worn and wrinkled, and his hair was long and dirty. When he turned around, I saw why he did not sit with the others. The entire left side of his face was twisted and deformed, and the position of his facial muscles rendered his left eye 90 percent closed.

When he turned around, he did not make eye contact with me. Sadly, he had learned to avoid attention, preferring the pain of isolation to the horror of constant rejection. In an instant, my mind wandered to what his elementary school days must have been like. I imagined the countless times his classmates had made fun of him, excluded him from recess gatherings and games, and failed to invite him over to play after school. Tears welled up within me, but I dared not cry, for that would communicate pity to him, something I did not want to do.

That evening, I introduced Chris to Someone who would fill his heart with acceptance. During the next six months, I saw him change before my very eyes. Ten years later, I learned that Chris was married, serving the Lord in his church, and teaching in a public school. What an amazing transformation, from a shy and reluctant college student to a person who daily stands in front of a classroom! How did this unfold? I'll share the rest of his story in a moment. But it's important to recognize right now that a key component in Chris's marvelous change was applying the basic principle of this book: we can get good at life and that it's possible to experience kingdom living now.

Chris's amazing transformation began when he turned his life over to Jesus Christ. He attended my weekly Bible study, sat in the front row, and earnestly took notes. When he was only three months into his new life in Jesus, I challenged him to stand at a busy street corner on campus and hand out "underground" Christian evangelistic literature. I knew this would be threatening to him, for it would force him to trust Jesus with the body language of rejection of oncoming college students. But I knew he needed to practice trusting Jesus for acceptance and being comfortable with rejection. So practice he did. Over and over he handed out literature. Repeatedly, he practiced choosing to sit in the front at the weekly Bible study.

As he started forming the habit of exposing himself to the attention of others, I met with him for a discipleship appointment one afternoon, four months into his Christian life. "Chris," I said, "I think there's something Jesus wants you to trust Him with."

"What's that?" he asked.

"I believe the Lord wants you and another Christian brother to ask two of the sisters to go out on a dinner date." I knew he wanted to start relating to the sisters, but he was still afraid. Yet he trusted me. I wrote out a simple paragraph he could use to ask a Christian sister out for a date, and we practiced it repeatedly. He also practiced it in front of the mirror. Finally, he and another brother in the group worked up the courage to ask two girls out, and guess what? They accepted. And Chris had a wonderful time. I was privileged to watch the transformation of a young man take place before my eyes.

What made the difference in Chris's life? What set him in the right direction early in the game? Many things, of course. But one factor is of crucial importance because it is often left out of discipleship today, and it is badly misunderstood. Notice that I did not simply teach Chris about self-acceptance and challenge him to listen to wonderful praise music that would motivate him to feel good about himself. Both of these I did, but three things were central to his transformation: practice, practice, practice. It was his repeated practice of doing certain things that formed the habit of courage, which replaced the habit of withdrawal.

In the stories Klaus and I have shared with you, we have laid out some key principles that we've found helpful in getting good at life. The central one is the paradox we started with, which is Jesus' statement "For whoever wants to save his life will lose it, but whoever loses his life for me will find it" (Matthew 16:25). The attitude and actions of self-giving implied by that verse are not meant to be a one-time decision. They must be repeated over and over daily—through practice. If you take up this challenge—a dedication to humble self-giving in the manner of Christ, the practice of God's presence (whether through the Jesus Prayer, the pause button, or another method), the conscious intention of putting others first (especially those closest to you), the aim to embrace God's hiddenness and to trust in Him openly (even through anxiety or depression), the purpose of inviting one or more close friends into your life—we believe you will notice dramatic changes in yourself, just as I saw in Chris. We urge you to step out today on your path of getting good at life.

NOTES

CHAPTER ONE: TODAY'S CONFUSION ABOUT HAPPINESS

1. Dallas Willard, *Renovation of the Heart: Putting On the Character of Christ* (Colorado Springs, CO: NavPress, 2002), 113.

2. Quoted in Andrew Delbanco, *The Real American Dream* (Cambridge, MA: Harvard University Press, 2000), 106.

3. Quoted in Gary T. Amos, *Defending the Declaration* (Charlottesville, VA: Providence Foundation, 1989), 119–120.

4. C. S. Lewis, *God in the Dock* (Grand Rapids, MI: Eerdmans, 1994), 280.

5. *Webster's New College Dictionary* (Springfield, MA: Merriam, 1975), 882.

6. Philip Cushman, "Why the Self Is Empty," *American Psychologist* 45 (May 1990): 600.

7. For a more extended list, see J. P. Moreland, *Love Your God with All Your Mind* (Colorado Springs, CO: NavPress, 1997), chapter 4.

8. Martin E. P. Seligman, "Boomer Blues," *Psychology Today* (October 1988): 55.

9. See Christopher Lasch, *The Culture of Narcissism* (New York: Warner Books, 1979), esp. chap. 2.

10. Lasch, 262.

11. See Martin Seligman, *Authentic Happiness* (New York: Free Press, 2002).

12. Seligman, "Boomer Blues," 55.

13. Michael Levine, "Why I Hate Beauty," *Psychology Today* (July/ August 2001): 38–44.

14. For an excellent discussion of the classical notion of happiness, see Jean Porter, *Nature as Reason: A Thomistic Theory of the Natural Law* (Grand Rapids, MI: Eerdmans, 2005), 141–230.

15. John W. Gardner, *Excellence: Can We Be Equal and Excellent Too?* rev. ed. (New York: Norton, 1984), 175. Of course, Gardner is confused about to whom we owe our dedication, and he fails to note that we need to give ourselves to a true and important cause. A life aimed at being a good Nazi or the best checkers player would, obviously, be a life wasted.

16. Henri Nouwen, *In the Name of Jesus* (New York: Crossroad, 1989), 43–44.

CHAPTER TWO: GAINING HAPPINESS BY LOSING YOUR LIFE

1. John W. Frye, *Jesus the Pastor* (Grand Rapids, MI: Zondervan, 2000), 103.

2. Plato *Gorgias* 500c.

3. Plato *Laws* 661a-c.

4. For a useful discussion of *body* and *flesh,* see G. E. Ladd, *A Theology of the New Testament* (Grand Rapids, MI: Eerdmans, 1974), 464–475. *Flesh* may actually refer on occasion to a fleshly community, one that walks according to a legalistic adherence to the old covenant. But even in these cases of the corporate use of *flesh,* the term *sarx* is derivative of the ethical usage in reference to individuals. See Walter Russell, *The Flesh/Spirit Controversy in Galatians* (Lanham, MD: University Press of America, 1997).

5. See Dallas Willard, *The Spirit of the Disciplines* (San Francisco: Harper & Row, 1988), 154–192.

6. Henri Nouwen, *Reaching Out* (New York: Doubleday, 1986), 25.

7. For suggestions of retreat centers in the United States, see *A Place for God: A Guide to Spiritual Retreats and Retreat Centers* (New York: Image, 2002).

8. Richard Higgins, "Americans' Interest in Religion Is Shallow, Some Analysts Believe," *Orange County Register,* April 22, 1991, A8.

CHAPTER THREE: FORMING A TENDER, RECEPTIVE HEART

1. Jean-Paul Sartre, *No Exit* (New York: Vintage, 1989), 45.

2. For further information on spending time with God, see Klaus Issler, *Wasting Time with God: A Christian Spirituality of Friendship with God* (Downers Grove, IL: InterVarsity, 2001).

3. Gerald Hawthorne, *Word Biblical Commentary: Philippians,* Vol. 43 (Waco, TX: Word, 1983), 184.

4. Hawthorne, 185.

5. Gerald May, *Addiction and Grace: Love and Spirituality in the Healing of Addictions* (San Francisco: HarperSanFrancisco, 1988), 11.

6. Dallas Willard, *The Divine Conspiracy: Rediscovering Our Hidden Life in God* (San Francisco: HarperSanFrancisco, 1998).

7. Clint Arnold, *Three Crucial Questions About Spiritual Warfare* (Grand Rapids, MI: Baker, 1997), 88–89.

8. Charles Kraft, *Defeating Dark Angels: Breaking Demonic Oppression in the Believer's Life* (Ann Arbor, MI: Vine/Servant, 1992), 120.

9. R. T. France, "The Gospel of Mark," *The New International Greek Testament Commentary* (Grand Rapids, MI: Eerdmans, 2002), 366.

10. John Nolland, *Luke 9:21–18:34*, *Word Biblical Commentary*, Vol. 35B (Dallas: Word, 1993), 505.

11. Gerald Wilson, *The NIV Application Commentary*, Vol. 1, *Psalms* (Grand Rapids, MI: Zondervan), 778.

12. Wilson, 778.

13. Wilson, 779.

14. For further information about divine guidance and hearing God, see Dallas Willard, *Hearing God* (Downers Grove, IL: InterVarsity, 1999), and chap. 6 in Klaus Issler, *Wasting Time with God: A Christian Spirituality of Friendship with God* (Downers Grove, IL: InterVarsity, 2001).

CHAPTER FOUR: FORMING A THOUGHTFUL MIND STAYED ON GOD

1. See R. M. French, trans., *The Way of a Pilgrim* (San Francisco: HarperCollins, 1965).

2. D. A. Carson, "Matthew," in *Expositor's Bible Commentary*, ed. Frank E. Gaebelein (Grand Rapids, MI: Zondervan, 1984), 166.

3. William Law, *A Serious Call to a Devout and Holy Life* (1728; Grand Rapids, MI: Eerdmans, 1966), 2. For a fuller treatment of the topic of this section, see J. P. Moreland, *Love Your God with All Your Mind* (Colorado Springs, CO: NavPress, 1997).

4. Dallas Willard, *The Spirit of the Disciplines* (San Francisco: Harper & Row, 1988), 156.

CHAPTER FIVE: FORMING A TRUSTING WILL THAT RISKS WITH GOD

1. "If a talent was worth six thousand denarii, then it would take a day laborer twenty years to earn so much—perhaps three hundred-thousand dollars. On any reckoning NIV's footnote ('more than

a thousand dollars') is much too low." D. A. Carson, "Matthew," in *The Expositor's Bible Commentary*, ed. Frank E. Gaebelein (Grand Rapids, MI: Zondervan, 1984), 516.

2. Carol Genengels, "Mother's Day Gift," in *Stories for the Spirit-Filled Believer*, ed. Christine Bolley (Lancaster, PA: Starburst, 2001), 279–281 (names have been changed).

3. G. K. Beale, *The Book of Revelation: A Commentary on the Greek Text (The New International Greek Testament Commentary)* (Grand Rapids, MI: Eerdmans, 1999), 1120.

4. C. S. Lewis, *Christian Behavior* (New York: Macmillan, 1945), 55.

5. Dawn Raffell, "Guiding Signs," in *Unsolved Miracles,* ed. John Van Diest (Sisters, OR: Multnomah, 1997), 49.

6. "Tutankhamen," *Encyclopedia Britannica Online,* www.britannica.com.

7. That we will learn in eternity is suggested by Ephesians 2:7: "So that in the ages to come He might show the surpassing riches of His grace in kindness toward us in Christ Jesus" (NASB). For a brief discussion of this topic, see Gary Habermas and J. P. Moreland, *Immortality: The Other Side of Death* (Nelson, 1992), 146.

8. Jim Elliot, in *The Journals of Jim Elliot,* ed. Elisabeth Elliot (Old Tappan, NJ: Revell, 1983), 174.

9. Dallas Willard, *The Spirit of the Disciplines* (San Francisco: Harper & Row, 1988), 175.

10. Michael Ryan, "Why?" *Parade Magazine,* September 21, 1997, 16.

11. Wallace Terry, "An Extraordinary Gentleman," *Parade Magazine,* November 9, 1997, 20–21.

CHAPTER SIX: EMBRACING THE HIDDENNESS OF GOD

1. I. Howard Marshall, "Commentary on Luke," in *The New International Greek Testament Commentary* (Exeter, U.K.: Paternoster, 1978), 897.

2. Piotr, in "The Dangerous Work of Evangelism," *The Voice of the Martyrs*, Special Issue, 2002, 16.

3. C. S. Lewis, *The Lion, the Witch and the Wardrobe* (New York: Macmillan, 1950), 75–76.

4. Brennan Manning, *The Boy Who Cried Abba: A Parable of Trust and Acceptance* (San Francisco: HarperSanFrancisco, 1997), 61–62.

5. Jack Deere, *Surprised by the Voice of God* (Grand Rapids, MI: Zondervan), 39.

6. Deere, 22.

7. Dallas Willard, *Renovation of the Heart: Putting on the Character of Christ* (Colorado Springs, CO: NavPress, 2002), 100.

8. Brother Lawrence, *The Practice of the Presence of God*, trans. Robert J. Edmonson, ed. Hal M. Helms (Brewster, MA: Paraclete Press, 1985), 126.

9. Cynthia Heald, "Experiencing God in the Day-to-Day," *Discipleship Journal* (January/February 1995): 58.

10. "Best Amazing Maritime Tale," *Parade Magazine*, December 29, 1996, 7.

CHAPTER SEVEN: DEFEATING TWO HARDSHIPS OF LIFE: ANXIETY AND DEPRESSION

1. "High Depression Rates Among Baby Boomers Pose Mystery to Experts," *The News and Daily Advance*, Lynchburg, VA, August 28, 1988.

2. Daniel G. Amen and Lisa C. Routh, *Healing Anxiety and Depression* (New York: Putnam, 2003), 1.

3. Holly Peters and Rob Westerveldt, "Silent Servants," *Biola Connections* (Spring 2004): 12.

4. Peters, 7–11.

5. See J. P. Moreland, *Love Your God with All Your Mind* (Colorado Springs, CO: NavPress, 1997), 53–56.

6. See Doc Childre and Howard Martin, *The HeartMath Solution* (San Francisco: Harper, 1999), chap. 1.

7. Childre, 71.

8. Childre, xv; compare 68–71.

9. For books documenting the ongoing presence of miracles throughout church history, see J. Sidlow Baxter, *Divine Healing of the Body* (Grand Rapids, MI: Zondervan, 1979), and Morton Kelsey, *Healing and Christianity* (New York: Harper & Row, 1973). For books recounting the miraculous, see Jack Deere, *Surprised by the Power of the Spirit* (Grand Rapids, MI: Zondervan, 1993), and *Surprised by the Voice of God* (Grand Rapids, MI: Zondervan, 1996); Jane Rumph, *Signs and Wonders in America Today* (Ann Arbor, MI: Servant Books, 2003); Sam Storms, *The Beginner's Guide to Spiritual Gifts* (Ann Arbor, MI: Servant Books, 2002); Peter Wagner, *Spiritual Power and Church Growth* (Lake Mary, FL: Creation House, 1986); and John Wimber, *Power Evangelism* (Anaheim, CA: Vineyard, 1985), and *Power Healing* (San Francisco: Harper, 1987).

10. One further aspect of depression involves the demonic. Unfortunately, we have neither the expertise nor adequate space to treat the demonic aspects of anxiety or depression, though this factor is critical for a truly holistic approach. For more on this

we suggest Charles Kraft, *Defeating Dark Angels* (Ann Arbor, MI: Servant, 1992). See also C. Fred Dickason, *Demon Possession and the Christian* (Wheaton, IL: Crossway, 1987), and Clint Arnold, *Three Crucial Questions About Spiritual Warfare* (Grand Rapids, MI: Baker, 1997).

CHAPTER EIGHT: CULTIVATING SPIRITUAL FRIENDSHIPS

1. J. I. Packer, *Concise Theology* (Carol Stream, IL: Tyndale, 1993), 42.
2. Aelred of Rievaulx, *Spiritual Friendship* (Kalamazoo, MI: Cisterican Publications, 1977), 74.
3. Mihaly Csikszentmihalyi, *Flow: The Psychology of Optimal Experience* (New York: HarperCollins, 1990), 189–190.
4. Aelred, 58.
5. Aelred, 103.
6. Dallas Willard, *The Divine Conspiracy* (San Francisco: HarperSanFrancisco, 1998), 147.
7. The following resources provide more information about developing friendships: of course, Aelred's *Spiritual Friendship*, as well as Gary Inrig, *Quality Friendship: The Risks and Rewards* (Chicago: Moody, 1981); resources related to personality differences: Bob Phillips, *The Delicate Art of Dancing with Porcupines: Learning to Appreciate the Finer Points of Others* (Ventura, CA: Regal, 1989); related to cultural differences: Duane Elmer, *Cross-Cultural Conflict: Building Relationships for Effective Ministry* (Downers Grove, IL: InterVarsity, 1993).

Academic resources include Paul Wadell, *Friendship and the Moral Life* (Notre Dame, IN: University of Notre Dame, 1989); Gilbert Meilaender, *Friendship: A Study in Theological Ethics* (Notre

Dame, IN: University of Notre Dame, 1981); a helpful secular study of the phases of friendship development by noted researcher Steve Duck, *Understanding Relationships* (New York: Guildford, 1991); a secular study specifically related to gender differences: Deborah Tannen, *You Just Don't Understand: Women and Men in Conversation* (New York: Ballentine, 1990).

8. John Wimber with Kevin Spring, *Power Healing* (San Francisco: Harper & Row, 1987), 70–71.

ABOUT THE AUTHORS

J. P. MORELAND is Distinguished Professor of Philosophy at Talbot School of Theology, Biola University, and director of Eidos Christian Center. He has written more than one hundred articles in magazines and journals and authored or coauthored over twenty books, including *Love Your God with All Your Mind* and *Smart Faith.* He has planted three churches and spoken on over two hundred college campuses and in hundreds of churches. He and his wife, Hope, have two married daughters, Ashley and Allison.

KLAUS ISSLER is Professor of Christian Education and Theology at Talbot School of Theology, Biola University. He has written two textbooks in the field of Christian education and one textbook on spirituality and formation, *Wasting Time with God.* He has taught seminars with Walk Thru the Bible, has served as a board member with an overseas mission agency, and is currently the book review editor of *The Christian Education Journal.* Klaus and his wife, Beth, have two adult children, Daniel and Ruth.

THINK ABOUT YOUR FAITH.

Smart Faith

Prepare your mind to love and worship God. J. P. Moreland and Mark Matlock sound a wake-up call to young believers who haven't fully explored the role of reason in the Christian faith.

Jesus told His disciples, "Love God with all your heart, soul, and mind." Consider this book Theology and Philosophy 101—here to help you love your God with all your mind. One of the only books of its kind, *Smart Faith* will sharpen your intellect and help you understand the reasons behind your faith in Christ.

J. P. Moreland and Mark Matlock
1-57683-734-3

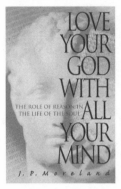

TRANSFORM YOUR SPIRIT.

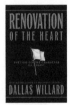